"Leithauser probably could have ... l the butterfly research he apparentl ...ning lightly . . . The irregularly rhy..... ... strict enough to strain out unnecessary detail but flexible enough to accommodate grand descriptive flourishes . . . *Darlington's Fall* is not just coherent, but *tight*."

—Eric McHenry, *New York Times Book Review*

"Leithauser has happily resolved the problem of making a unity between verse and fiction. The book is definitely a page-turner; the author's artful plotting holds the reader's curiosity. The period details are wonderfully convincing."

—Phoebe Pettingell, *The New Leader*

"Leithauser reveals astonishing inventiveness and flexibility . . . *Darlington's Fall* is extremely clever, yet its adroitness is more than matched by the risks of its narrative leaps and by its passion and humanity."

—Fredric Koeppel, *The Commercial Appeal*

"Essentially a love story, *Darlington's Fall* is also a fascinating meditation on chance, natural selection, the nature of science and art, the evolution of species—and the human individual."

—*Nature Conservancy*

"It's always fun to greet a book that's fresh and original . . . The rhyming strategy reflects wit and good sense . . . The slow, heaving, eons-long drama of geological time known as evolution creates a force field that keeps booming in our psyches long after we close *Darlington's Fall*. If that isn't a bookshopper's bargain, what is?"

—Peter Wolfe, *St. Louis Post-Dispatch*

DARLINGTON'S FALL

DARLINGTON'S FALL

A NOVEL IN VERSE

BY

BRAD LEITHAUSER

WITH DRAWINGS BY MARK LEITHAUSER

ALFRED A. KNOPF   NEW YORK   2003

THIS IS A BORZOI BOOK
PUBLISHED BY ALFRED A. KNOPF

www.aaknopf.com

Knopf, Borzoi Books, and the colophon are registered
trademarks of Random House, Inc.

Library of Congress Cataloging-in-Publication Data
Leithauser, Brad.
Darlington's fall: a novel in verse / Brad Leithauser.
p. cm.
ISBN 0-375-70944-4
1. Entomologists—Poetry.   2. Naturalists—Poetry.   3. Butterflies—Poetry.
4. Nature—Poetry.   I. Title.
PS3562.E4623 D3 2002
811'.54—dc21   2001045104

Manufactured in the United States of America
Published March 27, 2002
First Paperback Edition, September 20, 2003

For Mary Jo,

For whom I fell

The remotest discoveries of the Chemist, the Botanist, or Mineralogist, will be as proper objects of the Poet's art as any upon which it can be employed. . . . If the time should ever come when what is now called Science, thus familiarized to men, shall be ready to put on, as it were, a form of flesh and blood, the Poet will lend his divine spirit to aid the transfiguration, and will welcome the Being thus produced, as a dear and genuine inmate of the household of man.

—WILLIAM WORDSWORTH

The lavish profusion too in the natural world appals me, from the growths of the tropical forest to the capacity of man to multiply, the torrent of babies. . . . If we look at Nature alone, full of perfection and imperfection, she tells us that God is disease, murder and rapine.

—ALFRED, LORD TENNYSON

Greatest of all attempts to say one thing in terms of another is the philosophical attempt to say matter in terms of spirit, or spirit in terms of matter, to make the final unity. That is the greatest attempt that ever failed.

—ROBERT FROST

ARTIST'S NOTE

Thanks are owed to the Bogliaso Foundation and their Centro Studi Ligure, which provided my brother and me with a gracious and beautiful site for an initial month-long collaboration. And more than thanks are owed to my wife, Mary Bryan Leithauser, third partner in the collaboration, who always provided inspiration and sometimes guided the pencil.

M.L.

It's long, I know, for a poem (5,708 lines) but short for a novel (46,265 words, my computer tells me), and a novel's what I aimed to create here. I looked for dailiness and rootedness—for verse with the firm calendars and solid place names, the ingrained habits and the incremental persuasions and erosions, which the novel has typically found congenial. I wanted specificity. Although all characters within these pages—including the narrator—are fictions, in nearly every case I've tried to get the science right. (If the people are fabricated, I'd like to think the insects are genuine.)

A word about method, for those interested in verse mechanics. Having permitted myself rhymes that fall catch-as-catch-can, I vowed that nearly every line would have an exact, or perfect, rhyme. I've eagerly made exception, though, for those irregular rhymes I often prefer to "perfection": especially rime riche (prays/praise) and pararhymes or rim rhymes (please/applause).

With the publication of this book I find myself approaching my fiftieth birthday. It was nearly thirty years ago that I published my first poem, in *Poetry*, and looking back over the decades I see just how lucky I was to encounter, as friends and guides at the outset, a number of gifted poets whose lives happened to cross mine before they passed away: William Alfred, Elizabeth Bishop, Amy Clampitt, Robert Fitzgerald, James Merrill. . . . Any tribute to such a group will inevitably look inadequate, but even so this book goes out to them with fondest thanks.

B.L.

Contents

Darlington's Fall

In time he came to see his life
As borne by a pair of wings unequal to the weight
Of all his dreams. He fell. First air, then leaves,
Slipping, branches that might have held him, snapping instead,
And he hit the ground, and tumbled down a hole,
Through a rib cage opened like a tomb,
Somersaulting over buried family lives,
Towns, taxonomies, down, the scattered wrecks
Of outsize extinctions, and reached the salt shores of Hell,
And kept falling. He came to rest in time
On another shore—his own—and stood,
And walked, and watched the sun in disbelief
Dance on the gray-hearted sea, the moon lay a white
Soothing hand upon the broken rocks.

Half an Orphan

The hand hungers: the jewel of the world,
And his for the taking. In all his long
Life of looking, never once beheld
A thing so fine—never wanted anything
Quite so much as this astonishing
Being, this stout green glittering
Prize . . . But the getting his hands on it,
The business of the capturing,
That will be dicey (difficult, delicate),
With so many ways everything can go wrong . . .

Hands are hungry and with hungry hands
You must work extra hard to keep
Your wits about you, to be slow and quick
At once, as the situation demands.
(When you're so full of wanting, it's no small trick.)
    Boil down all the trees in the forest until
They form a single cup of resin, still
You would never concoct a green
So bright, so dark, so dizzyingly deep
As this, the purest color he has ever seen.

The jewel of the world: conceived
In mud and muck, then dropped on a fallen log
Down at the edge of the pond. He can't stop
Even to remove his shoes—no time—
Wades rights in, feet sucked at by the slime . . .
The trouble here? It's that the frog
(The hugest frog in all the world) can get away
So many different ways, can simply drop—
Flop!—and be gone, never to be retrieved.
Oh, so many ways for things to go astray!

He slides toward it, heart about to burst
In his mouth, heart full in his hands. *It must be
A dream* . . . that's what he'd thought at first,
Spotting it: so big, so green, and *right there.*
That was the amazing thing: the thing's reality.
The wish formed instantly, deep as any prayer:
Let me get my hands on him! Here's the prize
He's waited all his life for: the overfull
Eyes and barrel chest, the kingly receding skull,
The bulging banked power in the thighs . . .

A sliding step—a sliding step—and nearly
Nearly there. Inside his chest, desire suspends
A weight, a weight connected to a spring,
His heart like a mousetrap, waiting
To snap shut with an absolutely desolating
Empty *clap* . . . How will he bear it if the thing
Escapes?—oh, when he wants it so dearly,
Never wanted anything so much!
And almost there, now he can all but touch—
A hungry beggar's hand extends . . .

He lunges, just as the frog leaps,
And right there,
        in midair,
                in midair's where
The two creatures (hands of the one, brute
Miraculous torso of the other) lock
Together, a solid thumping *shock*
That races up his arm like a flare,
Crackles and cleanses and expands
As it climbs, torching his brain. (And the fire keeps
Burning: decades hence, when his fleet-foot
Boyhood's dim, he'll recall, with tingling hands,

The summer morning when his little hands
Clamped on the creature and held it whole,
Feeling in that moment so rich a press
Of feeling, perhaps no other touch
(Or maybe one?—one only?—the one to come
Four decades on?) ever will thrill him quite so much.
Oh, every cell in his body understands
What he himself cannot begin to guess:
This instant lasts forever, there are some
Encounters that configure your soul.)

The thing squirms—

                  squirms half loose, slips,
But his fingers **grapple**: one leg, *got* it, one
Big back leg grasped tight, as his other hand, scooping
Upward, catches it from below, grips
It round the chest: the booming noble pulse
Yes in his palm: he *has* it, it's now his great good luck
To *have* it: the jewel of the world—and where else
But in the warm chalice of his hands? A whooping
Howl rips free of his throat, winging like a duck
Over the trees, straight at the sun.

... Quite a specimen himself, striding in glory
From the swamp to Great Elm Street with his live
Plunder, feeling on this day of his greatest fame
Like king of the whole town, his hometown, Storey,
Indiana—this Russel Darlington,
Customarily known as Russ, although the name
He himself secretly prefers is one
Provided by Mr. Hauser, the town pharmacist,
Who calls him Little Mister Naturalist.
Russ is seven, this summer of 1895.

Quite a small boy still, yet even so
An object of large and labored supposition
To his neighbors. For one thing, his father, John,
May well be the county's wealthiest man; for another,
The boy's clearly in need of female supervision,
His mother having died three years ago
Giving birth to a stillborn son
(It being a truth universally understood
That a young male heir to a good
Fortune is in want of a mother).

Furthermore, there's the suspicion
That the boy's a little *odd*—that his passion
For caterpillars and beetles and worms,
For every gruesome godforsaken thing that squirms
Or slithers, skitters or creeps, goes well
Beyond anything you'd call typical;
No, he gives every sign, this proud possessor
Of a microscope and a chemistry kit,
Of being that thing so alarming whenever it
Appears in a slip of a child: a born professor.

Even so, nothing but warmth and joy
Attend him on his triumphal march through town. Russ
Puts his pop-eyed captive on display,
Reveling in the stooping notice of the men,
The sighing envy of every boy,
Assorted squeals from the girls. His pride
In having ventured a long way
Into the swamp and come out victorious
Helps quell the inner voice that warns, *When
I get home, she's going to tan my hide.*

She being strong-armed, steel-haired
Mrs. Agnes Houlihan, the complete
Housekeeper, rolling into one the roles of governess,
Accountant, and bouncer in the Darlington manse
On Haydn (pronounced Hayed-in) Street.
She always says, *A good boy shows it in his dress,*
And here he comes with sloshing shoes, swamp-stinky pants.
She's going to murder me, he whispers and, scared,
Cradles up against his muddy shirt
That warm live thing, his other heart.

... And she is something of a specimen
Herself, the widow Mrs. Houlihan,
Who rarely speaks of her late mate, and when
She does, dependably adds, "He was a no-good man"—
A woman who, in her surpassing rectitude,
Daily contends with a host of enemies:
Dust, drunkenness, idleness, seafood,
Underdone meat, mold, uppity tradesmen, dirty hands,
Waxy ears, women with no sense of shame, dungarees,
Dogs, dumbbells, do-nothings (the list expands).

An unusual woman—an unusual household:
The plump but square-boned matron clucking
Admonishments at a world whose lazy
Delinquencies daily manage to astonish her
Anew; the jittery-chattery small
Pale boy, so bright-eyed as to wind up looking
Congenitally feverish; and the tall
Taciturn dark-dressed father, lost in the fold
Of his distant thoughts and a billowing blur
Of pipe-smoke that leaves them all a little hazy.

It's as if clouds surround him on the bluest,
Crispest winter day, a man destined to remain
A figure of impenetrable feelings—
The widower John Darlington, making his way
Down Great Elm Street in black greatcoat and gray
Felt hat, constantly abstracted and yet
So remarkably shrewd in all his dealings,
Off now at a fast clip on his newest
Mysterious errand—to the bank, the train
Station, the town registry, the *Gazette* . . .

The complicated nature of his hold
On the townspeople's imagination
Is partly a matter of power and riches,
As he buys them up—quietly, without a stir—
Little lot by lot; partly his warm-and-cold
Formality (addressing shop-boys in knee-breeches,
Negroes, drunks on stoops alike as *sir*);
Partly the notion that, in his taciturnity,
Anything he bares about himself will be
Gleaned only through the closest observation;

And partly the result of his unsettling link
To the darkest collusions of the heart,
To the anxious ancestral intimacies
Of communal life—given that the Darlingtons,
A generation back, made their start
With a funeral home, founded by John Sr., John's
Father (tying them forever to bodies that bore
The traces of a hidden hunger for
Morphine, or a lifelong taste for drink;
Bodies scarred by beatings, by covert surgeries;

Bodies in which some feverish sin
Of the flesh, burrowing to the light with a will
Of its own, burned holes from within;
And bodies haunted by the ghost
Of a trace of a hint of an unnatural ending).
And though, these days, another family runs
The establishment, the Darlington name still
Stands over the door and in people's minds; most
Decent Storey folk wouldn't consider sending
Their loved ones anywhere but "over to Darlington's."

In addition there's the fact (keenly known
To half the population, anyway) that for all
His dour severity, and his tendency to race
Shyly away rather than greet you, tall
John Darlington's a fine-looking man . . . so if there's
Something a touch eerie to the air he wears
Of being in constant mourning, grief has its own
Appeals—as does the notion that the right
Sort of woman conceivably might
Replant a smile upon John's face.

Meanwhile, she grows prettier year by year,
And younger too, that tragical child-bride
(That flower whose sole crime was the urge to bloom),
Fair Katherine Darlington, who died
In childbirth . . . dear Katie who was forever
Meeting life with a laugh in her throat, bringing cheer
To the downcast and the outcast—she whom
John with his dark clothes and long midnight walks
Eternally mourns, and whom he never
Mourns, of whom he never talks.

In Katie's place at table now sits one
Who waited upon it in former days,
Agnes Houlihan. But whether she plays
Servant or symbolic wife-and-mother,
John doesn't permit either himself or his son
To employ her Christian name. (This is another
Of those niceties of John's that seem to marry
Egalitarian ideals to a quiet, wary
Unease with a world that will not keep its distance—
He's for "separate but equal" in a novel sense.)

There are times, the three of them sitting down
To Sunday supper, the oak-paneled room aglow
With slow spring dusk light and a lilac breeze,
When they might well be taken for
A happy household—the boy running on
About box turtles or ants or honeybees,
Mrs. Houlihan recounting, with a gloating frown,
Her victory over a thieving butcher, gaunt John
Abandoning his food to take up once more
The soaring solaces of pipe tobacco—

And times when an air of desperation might
Be discerned, as if the conscientiously
Polished silver, the flowers, the linen
Tablecloth, the starched napkin in every lap
(The tending to all those feminine
Civilities that men are apt to slight),
Bespoke an implicit vacancy,
The presence of an absence: the lost hand
Of the true wife and mother who, leaving the land
Of the living, left a hole too big to gap.

It's a long-term vacancy, one that nobody
Will ever fill—as Agnes alone knows
Even while the rest of the town may ask,
When will John Darlington finally unbend
And take a second wife?
                                    She remembers those
Nights after Katie's death when, mad for relief,
John the teetotaler barred the door to the study
And wouldn't emerge till he'd downed an entire flask
Of bourbon, painfully pursuing some end
To his pain, some answer to his grief—

A rattled, clanking search that went on
Night after night in that poisonous den
Of his, smoke so thick a soul could hardly draw
Breath, tumbling rivers of raw
Liquor knocked back without benefit
Of ice or water . . . until the evening John
Finally called her in, his eyes lit
With an unanesthetizable pain,
Voice a cold, an icy slur,
And made confession: "You know, I killed her"—

Killed her yes with his insistent need
To load her with another child, that mastering drive
At bottom nothing but a masculine greed,
Overriding all the doctors' good advice,
Who warned (Russ's delivery having left her wan,
Drained, ripped apart—no more than half alive)
She mustn't go through the ordeal twice.
This time? John finished the job he'd left half done.
    And for her part, Mrs. Houlihan
Understood his guilt, all his failings as a man,

Glimpsed them with a simplicity of sight
Forfeited by a modern world increasingly
Tempted to regard the mind as some immense
Labyrinth in which all questions of right
And wrong must first negotiate a hall
Of mirrors—reflection layered upon re-
flection, cause upon cause, in such a dense
Assembly of motivations that all
Sense of sin itself eventually is lost:
Yet it was a terrible thing, a man's lust.

It was Russel, right after his mother died,
Who entered a period of being half drowned
In tears; when asked to wash his hands, he might get
No farther than the kitchen, where, hidden inside
The pantry, he would (such a small boy) quietly set
To weeping . . . A month of this, before he found,
Underneath his quilt, a new pastime: hours
And hours with a handful of lead soldiers—
Attack and counterattack in a shadowy campaign,
The close-fought Battle of the Counterpane.

But then his life's path took another twist:
One blue day, he laced up his shoes, and, all bright eyes
And laughter-leaking grin, went bounding
Out-of-doors, a little man-in-motion:
Prising up stones for grubs and beetles, rooting
Into anthills, chasing after dragonflies,
Wading for tadpoles, climbing trees and looting
Birds' nests . . . a metamorphosis as astounding
As any worm-to-butterfly, this eclosion
Of Russ Darlington, Boy Naturalist.

In truth he seemed (to his father's anxious gaze)
Not merely recovered but altogether
Better than before—brighter, happier, far more
Full of life—though you might ask whether
All the sunny explorations of his days
Were paid for in full when he went to bed,
Where, all too frequently, the boy was visited
By wailing nightmares. Recurrently
Those dreams of his led him to an ocean shore
(This Indiana boy) with a rising sea,

And a half-flooded cave, or den,
Where monsters hid. (Well, one didn't need to be
Sigmund Freud—whose *Dreams* would not
Awaken the world for a few years yet
And wouldn't reach Storey until, oh,
Late into the twentieth century, and then
Principally in the form of talk-show
Self-help therapists—to see
What troubled Russ wasn't fear of the cave
So much as fear of the grave.)

Likewise, without any help from Vienna,
Or even William James's Cambridge,
The townsfolk made the link between
A family calling dedicated
To sprucing up corpses (powder for the nose,
Rouge for the cheek) and the boy's keen
Passion for insect-collecting, his rows
Of specimens laid out to best advantage—
Wing and mandible and antenna
Outspread on a heavenly cotton-wool bed.

Yet while the boy himself saw no link
Between the family's undertakings and his own,
He knew without doubt which of all his pleasures
Constituted his gravest residual sin:
His habit of removing the key from the chink
Beside the one detachable hearthstone,
Proceeding to his father's desk, tenderly
Sliding open the bottom drawer, reaching in,
And lifting out the jewel-encrusted box where she
Formerly housed her "treasures."

He adores the feel of them in his hands,
Loves to squeeze the milky pearls against the balls
Of his fingertips, tease the fine gold strands
Across his lips and bridgeless nose, set
A gem in his palm and conjure a magnificent
Summer palace of tinted, translucent
Rooms—whole lives lived behind those crystal walls!
He'd swear it: something even yet
Of her eyes' looking lingers in coign and facet,
And even something of her scent.

Each of her jewels he knows, each by its name,
For that was part—once, long ago—of a little game
The two of them shared. *Mommy, tell me:*
What's this? A ruby. *This?* Opal. *And this?* Cat's-eye.
And this is topaz, isn't it? Now aren't you clever . . .
And this? That's malachite. *This?* That one's my
Favorite, it's called watermelon tourmaline.
See?—just like watermelon, pink and green?
Except it's hard. Hard? Stones have to be,
You Little Tenderfoot. That's why they last forever.

And where is this one from? The beryl?
From Burma maybe. That's where you
Go to hunt tigers. *And this?* I think from Brazil.
What's there? A huge rainforest, with big blue
Parrots. And army ants. *I'd like that.* You know, my pet,
I think you would . . .
                              Men for her sake
Had swum shark-patrolled lagoons, trekked desert sands
(Home to the scorpion and rattlesnake),
Climbed glaciers, chopped through jungle—all to set
Gemstones upon her neck and hands.

Inside the box, each brooch, locket, earring, ring
Has its own special satin-lined niche, its own
Little home, and he never changes anything.
(He brings to its contents the same care
That will serve him so well in his later career:
An unteachable, bred-in-the-bone
Love of minute classification.) He knows
Even with his eyes shut where each stone goes:
Everything lies just exactly where it lay
The last time she put her jewels away.

... Until: comes a day he finds the key,
Opens the drawer, draws out carefully
The jeweled box of jewels, raises the lid,
And finds—

             finds one of life's great surprises:
The stones have shifted places. But how can this *be,*
When nobody else knows where the key's hid?
   The skin on the back of his neck starts to crawl ...
Surely—yes surely some ghost's responsible,
It's part of some ghostly prank.

                      Then he realizes
(And this? Oh, the strangest thing of all—

And a secret he *must never tell*)
Realizes exactly what this means:
Someone else, there's someone else can't stay
Away from Momma's jewels—comes and unlocks
The bottom drawer, withdraws the box,
Selects a few stones and warms them in his hand;
Someone else who maybe also leans
His face down full into their richness and,
Greedily, draws from the bright stone bouquet
A faint, fresh, imperishable smell.

The Advantage of Reality

(1898–1905)

Russel's back in the jungle once again . . .
Scarcely matters where he starts (a pew
At church, his desk at school, a trip
Downtown with Mrs. Houlihan, a visit to
The dentist, Dr. Doane), his imagination slides
Away, leaves thicken, a handful of monkeys slip
Through the dark understory, a burly serpent glides
Headfirst down a bearded tree, the bullying cry
Of a macaw whips across the sky . . .
It's 1898, and Russ is ten.

His favorite novel of all time? It's time's loophole,
Arthur Conan Doyle's *The Lost World,* or would be
Were it written yet. (It will seize his soul
Twenty years from now; he'll undergo
A happy dwindling, stepping forth as ten-year-old Russ
Into a relict land where dinosaurs roam free.)
But mostly he prefers nonfiction. Where's the sense
In made-up folks and fabricated incidents,
When he can supply all those himself? No,
Fact is good enough when the world's miraculous.

The books he loves best are the accounts
Of men who lit out for the darkness, off
To chronicle the world's wonders where
The world's most wondrous: in the jungle. It's there
You find fur-coated spiders the size
Of dinner plates, thumb-sized birds, beetles that pounce
On mice, rats that climb trees, fish that climb trees, ants
That farm mushrooms, termitary mounds large enough
To house, like Chicago, two million inhabitants,
And the brightest, biggest butterflies.

The jungle (so he's read) can be a place of horror—
Diseases to swell up your feet as round
As your head, slinking parasites that lay
Crackly eggs beneath your skin, worms that will enter
Your body through *any* hole whatever, snakes
That squeeze you till your backbone breaks . . .
But the man who makes his way home from there can say,
I have ventured to the world's pulsing center
And heard it echo like a drum. The richest sound
In all the world? That's easy: *explorer*.

He owns their books, he is their secret son—
Richard Spruce, *A Botanist on the Amazon;*
H. W. Bates on the Amazon; Thomas Belt
In Nicaragua; Baron von Humboldt
Tracking the jungle from the mountains to the sea;
Russ's middle-namesake Alfred Russel Wallace
In the Malay; and Darwin's *Voyage,* where he writes,
"Brazilian scenery is nothing more nor less
Than a view in the Arabian nights,
With the advantage of reality."

In a vacant lot at the edge of town,
Russel is back in the jungle once more . . .
Under a lilac branch, he has turned up a sprawling
Anthill, and it's enough—off in an instant, he's gone.
The ants become Mayan slaves, hauling
Stones up a pyramid. A gold dandelion serves for
Sun, and a white windblown dandelion
For the waning moon. The ants erect temples to
The unimaginable Gods, those creatures who
Look down from the heavens as he's now looking down.

This has occurred before, may occur again:
For days on end a man hacks and pulls
His way through all but impassable foliage
And suddenly breaks in upon a buried palace—
All the slumped splendor and deep, cryptic labors
Of a once-flourishing and now forgotten age:
Tombs, tumbled temples, stelae and great stone skulls,
The whole complex buried under *matapalos,*
Those tree-killing trees that strangle their neighbors . . .
All but buried under centuries of rain.

But *this*? *This* is a miracle on the wing:
Nothing like—

                nothing ever anything
Like this before: in this lot on the edge of town,
Arrives a miracle:: a god: a goddess: down
From heaven he/she/it appears, chancing to rest
For one stunned moment on his shirtsleeve . . .
His jaw hangs slack: impossible to believe:
Yet here it is   what couldn't be   upon his wrist::
The world's most beautiful butterfly: a thing
Whose colors go well beyond astonishing . . .

Off—and she's away, for a moment making right
For Heaven, though he's off after, net in hand, flung
Headlong, lunging for her as she swoops low
For a dandelion, as she flutters among
Some fern-fronds (but again no luck),
And as she gives the lilac a second look
(And now—careful!—for she really *is*
Too big for his small net) (which must close oh
So gently, creating a lantern for the light
Of the world—*which now is his!*).

He knows how to hold a butterfly—a good thing,
Because otherwise they'll batter and fight
In your cupped hands until the wings are ground
To tatters and powder . . . No: just
Index finger and thumb, and not too tight;
A simple clamp on the thorax, let each wing
Beat and flutter as if still in flight . . .
There's a fine pressure to be found
Between the maiming and the maintaining;
It's a matter, as much as anything, of trust.

He takes the back way back home, exultant and yet
Reluctant to share his prize, to exhibit
Or explain . . . She'll be more guest than pet
In his biggest, gallon glass jar, with a spread
Of flowers to feed on, fresh leaves for a bed,
Plenty of airholes punched in the metal lid: *she*
Will never lack for anything. Nobody
In all of Indiana, he would bet,
Nobody in Storey (of this, he feels sure)
Has ever made so amazing a capture.

Only after she's been seen to in every detail
(Lapped in luxury, with big banks
Of blooms and leafage, and a brimming thimble-pail
Of sugar water) does he take from the shelf
A choice possession, *The Butterfly Book*
By W. J. Holland, though with little hope
Of locating *her* in its ordered ranks
Of specimens—hardly the place to look
For one so clearly beyond the scope
Of all guidebooks, someone so purely herself.

Or she's a new species, lacking the name
That he alone, sole discoverer, is to bestow.
    Henceforth, his life can never be the same—
A fact not immediately registered
By Mrs. Houlihan (who frowns on bringing bugs
Of *any* sort into the home, somehow seeing no
Distinction between butterflies and ticks, wasps, slugs),
Nor to Daddy, who does mumble an approving word,
While puffing on his pipe, yet who seems today
More than usually far away.

Still, what else is there to talk about
Than the urgent responsibility of finding out
(There must be *some* book, *some* person they could ask)
Just what she is, and where she might
Have come from? Far more than curiosity's
At stake here—it's a matter of *right:*
For she deserves the dignity of a name, and he's
The only one, evidently, to get the job done;
He has no doubt it's the weightiest task
The world ever assigned Russel Darlington.

When, the third morning, Russ finds her folded in
The bottom of the jar, dwindled, like a little
Party-favor someone's thoughtlessly shed,
He's ready. (Butterflies usually don't live long.)
Now's the time, before she turns too brittle,
To open her out and lay her on the cotton bed
He's already made up, fix her on her pin,
Seal her behind glass—safe in her strong,
Airtight, and insectproof new home.
She'll stay in his room; she's going to live with him.

Well, she may be dead but he's in no way freed
From his responsibilities—to the contrary:
It's all the more urgent, now that she's lying
In a fancy but unmarked grave, to find out who
She really is. So Russ rattles on, without
Quite knowing what he expects his father to do,
Or even if Daddy hears: *There's no denying*
She's something rare . . . This is no ordinary
Butterfly . . . Maybe a whole new species . . . We need
To find out the truth about her—need to find out . . .

Russel is desperate. And persistent.
And it turns out Father *has* been listening,
All along—at dinner announcing that on Saturday
The two of them will be journeying
To Old U, to consult a "real expert," who may
"Provide the necessary information."
(The "Old U"? The mind of John Darlington
Admits only one source of higher education,
The university in Remington—
His alma mater, some thirty miles distant.)

And so it happens one Saturday
In the month of June, 1898,
Early in the morning, father and son and son's
Careful assembly of prize specimens
(Including she who is most prized of all)
Board a train. Airplanes this morning are as far away
As pterodactyls, but a new century's just
Around the corner. On small farms corn grows tall,
And horse-and-buggies in clouds of slowly settling dust
Halt for the huffing train bearing Russel to his fate.

*

They're met at the station by Father's friend,
Dean Buchman, whose name doubly misleads Russ
(He takes Dean for the man's Christian name,
And imagines Buchman spelled B-O-O-K).
The Dean's booming laugh unsettles him, as does his way
Of slapping things (a bench, his knee), but in the end
Such jollity's something to be grateful for:
It encourages Father to join in a game
Of trying to match joke with joke—a boisterous,
Boyish joshing Russ never saw before.

The old friends settle into an office where
Towers of smoke go up in a hurry
(Dean Buchman, too, adores his pipe), and, lost in their
Chatter and laughter, they leave Russ all but
Forgotten in a corner. No harm done.
He's happy. There's something familiar but strange,
Old and new and *comforting* in this change
In Daddy, tones of laughter warm and blurry
As the loop of sun on the rug at their feet. There's—what?
A secret there, somewhere, in the blinding sun.

(Dean Buchman—who is he? A man whose delight
On this June morning is heartfelt. He's relieved to see
His old friend Darlington in good condition
After that tragedy with his wife—hadn't there been
Rumors of a collapse? And pleased to connect again
With someone who has steadily accrued, despite
A reputation for stiff Lincolnian honesty,
One of the largest fortunes in the state—
Just the sort of man a dean of vision
At a growing university must cultivate.

John, too, is heartened in a way he'd not foreseen—
To be back in this place where he was once
So happy, so young. He's keen to revisit all
The old sights, catch up on what they now call
The scuttlebutt, get the lowdown from the Dean
About these plans for expansion . . . Oh he's
Already, unwittingly, gravitating toward
That position he'll accept in a few months:
John Darlington, member of the Board
Of the University Trustees.)

Eventually, Russ is fished from his quiet
Pool of daydreams in the blinding
Loop of sun and called to the inner circle of smoke.
He's asked to make some account of himself—which he does.
Father then clarifies their errand: they're here because
Russ, who "lives in the swamp" (another joke
From Daddy, who today won't stop joking), went and caught
A "spectacular butterfly," which he brought
Here with him this morning in hopes of finding
"Some expert who maybe could identify it."

The Dean brightens. "You've come to the right place!
John, we've got one of the best butterfly men
In the country. But I must say"— a cloud on his brow—
"He's a pretty odd duck. An Austrian. And"—
More clouds—"he may scare the boy." "Scare him? How?"
"It was a childhood accident. Kicked in the face
By a horse. Afraid he's a bit of a fright."
John Darlington ponders a moment and then,
As happens when *matters of principle* are at hand,
Lifts his chin: "Disfigured? Russ'll handle that all right."

A walk across campus. A flight of stairs. A knock
By the Dean on a red door. And a man with a bent
Face like a slab of meat jammed into a too-small pot.
One eye a pale blue. And the other? Not
An eye but a pearl onion, cloudy gray. Professor Schrock.
"Russ, shake hands." Russ shakes. The errand is made clear,
And Russ at last removes the paper he'd wound
Round the wooden frame. And now the sound
Above all others Russ has longed to hear:
A gasped intake of sheer thrilled wonderment.

"This was got locally?" (Actually: "Diss
Vuzz gaut . . ."—the Professor has quite an accent.) Yes. No.
In Storey. Father explains: "Thirty miles from here."
"Aaahh. Amazing. *Urania marina. Very* queer."
It's a—"A diurnal moth." A moth—not a butterfly!
Of course, of course—just look at the antenna!
Russ in his dazzlement had never stopped to ask why—
But Schrock says, "This one's a tropical. Mexico.
Jamaica." Then how did it get to Indiana?
"Brought for a collector—hmp? As a chrysalis?

And escaped? Or a storm carried it as far
As Texas, and then maybe it rode north in a train car?
Extraordinary, in any case." And never seen
In Indiana? "In Indiana?" The Professor lets fly
A dog's bark of a laugh. "Hmp. I pose it with some
Confidence: you're the first one ever to find
Such as this in Indiana. It's—one of a kind."
And triumph circles the room—from Schrock's one good eye
To the boy, and from boy to father, and from
John Darlington to the Dean.

Dean Buchman: "Professor, perhaps you'd be willing
To show young Russ round the lab? Teach him a thing
Or two about this entomology business,
Where I'm told his future lies?" The Dean laughs buoyantly.
And Father adds, softly, "Would you like that, son?"
Like it? A prospect far too thrilling
To be spoken aloud. Nod nod nod—oh *yes yes yes!*
Which is how Russ winds up alone with the one-
Eyed overseer of what turns out to be
A treasury beyond all imagining.

The biggest bees, biggest crickets he's ever seen;
A walking stick that must be ten inches long;
And the beetles!—pink, baby blue, gold-dust green,
Some (you'd swear) made from porcelain, enamel, metal;
Others (just like a storefront) from wood and tinted glass;
Others (the softest) formed from leaf and petal.
Some meant to fade into the field, others bold as brass;
And damselflies fine as the line of a pen,
Torsos that are nothing but a wing and a song,
Just a big pair of angel-wings, dancing on a pin . . .

But nothing born of earth can rival the glory
Of the butterflies—creatures only to be conceived
On a night when Mother Nature lay dreaming
The deepest, brightest dream she ever knew:
No leaves so green as these, no skies so blue,
And creams and reds and purples, Glasswings and Morphos,
Birdwings and Metalmarks and Swallowtails retrieved
Within the collapsed cones of long-overgrown volcanoes
And the towering rainforest's gloomy understory,
From high, drought-cracked creek beds and steaming

Cypress swamps, stinking to high Heaven . . .
Wings white-spotted like dominoes, black-spotted like dice,
Patterned like new suits of playing cards, no two the same—
Wedge and Loop and Chevron, Swirl and Band . . .
    It's too much for Russ to take in, almost, even
As a voice keeps calling, from the belly of his soul,
More, please; more. He's led to a microscope—a device
That puts his own boxy Leitz to shame—
And tumbles, like Alice in the rabbit hole,
Down its tube, entering that Underland

Of mountainous minutiae
Where scientists go to pursue their research,
Where you can see how each scale-plate
Fits the *tormogen* (so the Professor calls it),
The doughnutlike sockets holding them in place;
And stare a luna moth in the face;
Even enter the dissected chest of the great
Migrator—the monarch butterfly—
To discover a space imposing as a church,
And a heart big as a pulpit.

And just the way a trudging, market-bound farmer might,
At the clattering arrival of his lord and king,
Proffer in tribute whatever humble thing
He bore on his back—a cheese packed in hay,
A sack of meal—Russ resolved that his pitifully slight
Collection should now be put on display
For the Professor: crickets, wasps, a terrapin,
A rabbit's tooth, the ghost-tube of a snakeskin—
Samples of the dun, dusty, diminished fauna
To be found round Storey, Indiana.

Then the conversation took a peculiar turn.
The Professor asked—This one, what date was it obtained?
Of course Russel didn't know. What hour
Of day? Russ wasn't sure. What sort of flower
Or bush was it captured on?

                              Uh—the bush? Russ explained
(Or tried to, under the dual burden of feeling
Somewhat overwhelmed and being only ten)
That it wasn't plants he was interested in,
Only butterflies. At which, the Professor grew stern
(Looked almost angry) and set about revealing

The numerous ways Russ had fallen short:
There's no excuse . . . Without supporting documentation
The specimens are useless—no good to anybody . . .
Because—because a butterfly lives inside
A *web*—a web of plants, of information . . .
You can't remove—my God!—These must be seen
Within the larger web . . . No one can study
Butterflies in isolation . . . You haven't even tried . . .
      And just as the Professor had worked up to a sort
Of tantrum, they returned, Father and the Dean.

Shaken by shame, chagrin, a touch of fear,
Russel was too confused to follow, quite,
Either the extricating goodbyes or the shared
Exchange of whispers in the hall
Afterwards ("John, listen, I feel bad
About this—" "Believe me, perfectly all right . . ."
"You must understand how it is, they're all all
A bit odd, these bug men—" "Quite"). But he felt clear
Relief when his father on the train home declared,
"We won't see *him* again. Schrock. The man is mad."

*

Farewell to the Professor? Yes, all right—
But goodbye to the room where the butterflies
Are stacked in drawers like banknotes in a vault?
And goodbye to the Goliath and the Emperor
The size of his fist? He's helpless to halt
The cravings, the visions they evoke . . . At night
The thought of Schrock's treasury keeps him awake
And he must—*must* get back there; it's a sort of ache
In the front of his head, this hunger in his eyes
To scrutinize them all once more.

No good to anybody and simply *no excuse*—
Just like that: Russ's finest jewels dismissed.
Utterly *no good to anybody* because
Of his failure to maintain a proper list,
With weather, date, the exact situation . . .
And yet, hurtful as those words remained, there was,
Russ now began to see, a rich kernel of sense
In them, as well as something better: an intimation
That a lone pursuit of bugs could be of *use*
(First inklings of a collegial audience).

Within a week, Russ was carrying a notebook
And a field guide to the local plants
When he went collecting; within two,
He was pleading for a return trip to Old U
And the Professor—pleas that (truth to tell) met with no
Strong resistance from his father . . . Another
Visit? So soon? Well—and why not? A chance
To do more catching up, perhaps have a look
At those expansion plans . . . and did you know,
Russ, that *alma mater* means Soul Mother?

This time, the Professor, projecting
Mixed signals from one moment to the next,
Began by not merely reviewing but *correcting*
The boy's notebook, in blood-red ink—but then
Gave Russ a gift, a book about biology,
And suddenly the boy's overjoyed . . .
At least until, on the train home, he actually
Tried to read what turned out to be a college text.
(A *madman,* John concluded, once again—
Somebody henceforth to avoid.)

Introduction to Biology—Russ was lost
By the bottom of the very first page.
It was hopeless. It made him want to cry. But
The next day he made a little headway.
The next, a little more. Slow and steady.
It's what the jungle must be like—a living cage,
Step by step, carve out a path for yourself, cut
And slash . . . He must take notes each day,
As the Professor advised, prepare a list
Of questions. This time he would be ready . . .

And how could John Darlington ever have guessed
That a struggle for his son's soul
Had already taken shape—that Russ had found here,
In the pull between home and laboratory,
His life's central tension? And *had* John been able
To recognize in Schrock the adversary
With whom he was destined, year after year,
To wage an undeclared war for control
Of the boy's future, wouldn't it be reasonable
To suppose that it must be no contest?

After all, what battle could be more one-sided?
   In this corner, John Darlington, who of course
Is not only father to the boy (with all the ties
Of love and loyalty which that implies),
But the boy's sole parent for the last five years.
Furthermore, there's the fact (though John prided
Himself on never "playing one of the big and great")
That he was, increasingly, a force
To be reckoned with, not only here
In Storey but throughout the State.

   In the far corner? The foreigner, face rearranged
By a horse's hoof; the raging man with the queer
Laugh and broken English, who hadn't enough self-pride
To wipe the food stains from his collar;
A man (as time went on, John made a few
Discreet inquiries) who had no friends and was estranged
From most of his colleagues, was much too
Fond of his beer, and lived in abject squalor.
This was a rival? What was there to fear
In a man who couldn't keep his own shoes tied?

Yes, what could be more one-sided? Since
John could offer only love and beneficence
And strength, wisdom and generosity,
Whereas Schrock had something else—he had butterflies.
He had his hands on the goods Russ was burning
To possess: not merely the drawers stocked with prize
Specimens (the prime attraction, initially),
But a uniquely intimate form of learning
Which becomes at last a way of looking, of putting
Biped and hexapod on an equal footing.

Schrock had the magic, he had the microscope,
He was the genie who could float you down
Until you stood, as on a flying carpet, upon
The tapestried dust of a butterfly's wing.
Schrock had the expertise, he had the tools,
He was the troll who knew the path
Into the mountain's core where the jewels
Of the world are plucked from a fiery bath,
And what mere mortal, father or not, could hope
To compete with the keeper of the molten spring?

*

Now an endless campaign begins, with one scene
Repeated over and over—Russel begs
For a return visit to his new mentor,
John protests of having too much work to do.
    The tide of battle turns when Russ turns thirteen,
Old enough, as long agreed, to journey to Old U
Alone, which he does most weekends, boarding
The train as weighted down with printed matter
As any Bible salesman. The Gospel according
To Schrock? Its prophets have antennae—and six legs.

It wasn't *healthy,* that was evident,
And yet the precise legal grounds by which John might
Curtail his son's journeys remained unclear.
How was Russ (now called a "lab assistant") being harmed?
Neglecting his studies? Hardly. Always the bright
Boy of the class anyway, he'd now begun, armed
With the discipline of Schrock's regime,
To surpass his classmates to such an extent
His teacher confessed to John, "I walk in fear
Of Russel's corrections"; nor did it seem

The boy was unhappy—not, in any case,
In the slouching and moody fashion
Typical of a discontented schoolboy.
No, not *unhappiness* John read in his son's face,
But worry, fear . . . though somebody else might conclude
Russ was one of those rare children who, having found
Their true calling at the outset, now are bound
To pursue it with a stringent, grown-up passion;
Someone might even say the kid bore his load
Of books with a feverish joy.

Still, it pained John to see his young son
Looking so much like an overborne
Little man, mumbling about his "work," stoop-
Shouldered and pale, showing so little interest
In sports or games or other *children* . . . One
Christmas, John asked him to compile a list
Of possible gifts, and what did Russ
Come up with? A typewriter, a new loupe,
A dissection kit, display cases, various
Entomology textbooks—and chloroform.

John accepted the notion, as only fair,
That the boy's oddities were his own fault—
Having failed to provide him with a mother's care,
Having so often walled himself up behind
Distant reveries . . . and failing too to call a halt
To Professor Schrock, who—completely out of his mind
And wily in his madness—worked each week to spring
Some new demand, climaxing in a request that Russ,
Age thirteen, be given private tutoring
In German—honestly! Of all the ridiculous . . .

(And yet in this matter too the lunatic
In time got his way—though it made John, who'd always
Recoiled at the sound of German, heartsick
To hear the boy, behind his bedroom door, laboring
To replicate the guttural glottal
Gruntings of that ugly tongue. But who
Could stand up to Russ, or deny him anything,
When he fixed on you that hurt, hopeful gaze?
He asked so little, really: just freedom to pursue
His passion at full throttle.)

And there was, too, John's anxiety
Over whether it mightn't be a grave mistake
To interfere with anyone quite possibly
Destined to soar far and wide
Over terrain nobody'd ever mapped before,
Before alighting in the history books beside
Leeuwenhoek, Darwin, Pasteur . . . What *was* in store
For such a boy? Who could say what fabulous form this
Omnivorous caterpillar of a child would take
By the final metamorphosis?

*

So John Darlington, temperamentally loath
To intrude on anyone, mostly stayed mum,
While praying that puberty would arrive
Soon and divert his son's attentions from
Six-legged specimens to those with two,
Meanwhile fretting (though well aware of what a fool
This made him sound) that somehow the boy (who
In stockinged feet stood only five feet five
On his sixteenth birthday) had stunted his growth
Through a devotion to the minuscule.

Long ago John had become reconciled
To never quite understanding the appeal
Of Russ's research (such small creatures, so immense
A load of nomenclature); and likewise had grown
Resigned to never having a sense
Of what constitutes success or failure in
So remote and specialized a discipline.
. . . Even so, it's a queer sensation to feel
That somehow the work of your peach-fuzz–faced child
Has become more *pressing* than your own.

All his mixed feelings are pushed to the fore
When Russ, now seventeen (and inching up—five-eight),
Begins to think of college. On the one hand,
What could be finer than if a son raised
Without a mother were to matriculate
At his father's alma mater?
                              Yet here was a chance
To pry Russ from Schrock and that crazed
Bug-morgue of a lab . . . Maybe, after all, John had planned
The wrong future for the boy: a change in atmosphere
Might be nothing less than a deliverance.

Hence, when Russ declared an intention to head east,
Perhaps to Cornell (distinguished birthplace
Of the world's first department of entomology),
Or Harvard (slower off the mark, but now the scene
Of an accumulating antlike industry),
Or Columbia (just up the road from
The country's finest natural history museum),
John felt some relief. He only asked (the least
That must be done) that Russ go explain, face-
To-face, his decision to the Dean.

So one foggy fall morning in 1905,
The trees on the Quad emerging in shades of rust
And flame, Russ winds up parrying compliments
With Dean Buchman (*We'd like nothing more* . . .
Of course I'm deeply . . . *Young men of your drive*
Are just what this . . . Of course I'm grateful for . . .
Special cases call for special . . . Oh, this place
Has been a home away from home since I was just . . .
Just so—you see I have a letter about your case
From Professor Schrock . . . Well, he's been an immense . . .),

Until Dean Buchman's called away by a secretary
And Russ, in a show of something like defiance,
Or at least a proprietary insouciance,
Rises and ambles to the window, studies the trees,
Strolls over to the Dean's desk where he—
Where his eyes fall upon—Schrock's letter . . .
It is, yes, it's a sort of taking stock,
A register of Russ's virtues and deficiencies
(The emphasis falling on the latter,
Needless to say, Schrock being Schrock).

Russ, racing down the page, now learns
That his Latin is "oftentimes incorrect,"
That he has neglected to work as hard
At his French and German as he should,
That his study of botany "shows scant returns,"
He "lacks patience" and "could be more methodical."
That while his mathematical skills are good,
He still has "a tendency to regard
Nature in a sentimental light"—oh, all
The qualifications you'd expect!

But there at the bottom of the page
The final paragraph is something else again,
Its phrases pumping powerful inebriants
Into Russ's veins: "Such reservations having been
Duly documented, nonetheless it is my view
That there is no other American of his age,
And perhaps no European, with a deeper
Knowledge about the Lepidoptera."
    Harvard? Cornell? Who needs them? What's the sense?
Russ will be matriculating at Old U.

OLD U

(1906–1910)

From his classmates, with all their wit-
Bristly banter and ritualized brotherly strife,
Their pranks and prayer meetings, feuds and loyal bands,
Their clandestine confabulations and great
Public utterances, he asked only to be
Left alone, content to circulate
On the edges of things, where they were equally
Content to have him, making no demands.
Not merely a workable arrangement—it
Was perfect! He'd never felt so pleased with life.

He'd reached the place where everything felt right;
He'd come *home,* coming to the University,
Where he was, in all ways, ideally outfitted—
Managing, with the Dean's connivance, to obtain
A room to himself, where he could work all night
(No roommates to disturb, nothing to explain),
And was given a key to the lab, permitted
To come and go just as he pleased, treated more
Like a professor than a student, and feeling, for
The first time in his life, absolutely free.

... Free to miss most meals (eating on the wing—
Apples, raisins, pickles, crackers, cheese,
Whatever needed no cooking and would keep
In his room without going bad), and free to fall asleep
In his clothes. Most of his classmates had no
Discipline, it turned out, simply didn't know
How to concentrate—flailing about while Russ
Floated down the stream, equally at ease
In physics, Latin, biology, calculus,
Garnering highest marks in everything.

The sole problem concerned his mother tongue: Eng. Comp.—
Oh, those weekly compositions were like pulling teeth!
What precisely are Samuel Johnson's views
On springtime or *on mendicancy*—and *do you agree?*
　　But what did it matter if Russ Darlington expressed
Disagreement with Sam Johnson? In the event, who's
The arbiter of right and wrong? Underneath
The floods of words, what empirical test
Could haul all such disquisitions out of the swamp
Of pure opinion? Where was objectivity?

And what to write about? What exactly to say?
In the end Russ went to his professor, who
Counseled, Look to your heart ... which sounded very nice,
But honestly why in the world look *there*
When any fool could tell you the heart's advice
Would just as soon mislead you as guide you true?
With each passing year, Russ felt less and less
Patience when asked to read a novel or a play,
Out of sorts with that queer writerly business
Of making people purely to make them bear

A load of burdens—burdens that the author,
If feeling generous, might lift in the final act ...
But look how much time's saved, right from the start,
If you don't compel nonexistent people to lay
Their overtaxed souls upon a page! In fact,
He wasn't all that fond of poetry either,
Which likewise failed to *progress*—though he'd come round
To a love of Wordsworth, a man who showed in his art
A reverence for Nature so profound
The words finally didn't get in the way.

God bless Doc Johnson, but how was any musing
Of *his* upon the world's wonders ever to compete
With the riddles of the soon-to-be imago
Sheathed in the ever more tenuous shell
Of the chrysalis—the wrap decrementally losing
Opacity as the wings' pigments filter through?
A different Sam (Coleridge) put it well,
Actually: Feed on the truth until it colors you
As the green leaf colors the insect. Just so:
The truth is *out* there . . . No more talk, let's eat.

Johnson could wait—he wasn't going anywhere.
But entomology *was,* and fast, and oh, what great
Good fortune to be a "bug man" in this age!
Better than he could describe it, Russ felt it in the air:
An advancing of breakthroughs in this,
The accelerated dawn of the new century:
The true birth of genetics (though "gene" hadn't yet
Been spliced off as a word); and soon—yes?—some synthesis
With Darwin's evolution, Man's mastery
Of the science of Man brought to a whole new stage!

To be a young man in a young field . . . Only now
This science of entomology, with its prize
Subdiscipline, the Lepidoptera, is beginning
To take wing. Only now, all of it banding
Together: embryology, taxonomy, mor-
phology, zoogeography . . . Since long before
The Greeks paid them the compliment of pinning
Their name to the very soul of man, butterflies
Have gripped the *psyche;* but now arrives the know-how
Needed to wed passion to understanding.

To be left alone by his classmates was all
He'd ever looked for, yet the start of his third year
A finer goal came into view: he could gain
Their admiration. This revelation broke
After the best summer of his life; so that, that fall,
It seemed the very planet might be—might be in love
With the process of unveiling an endless chain
Of blissful surprises. (He toyed with the notion of
An experimenting God, Himself none too clear
What would unfold the day the first caterpillar woke.)

The summer of '08, mentor and mentee,
A pair of "wing prospectors," went west, traveling
As far as Preid's Gulch, Idaho, on ever more
Raw stretches of rail track, there at last
To wander the mountains. (Not as much wandering,
In truth, as Russ would've liked; Schrock the naturalist
Was no outdoorsman.) Ten days set aside
For camping, collecting . . . and on the seventh Russ spied,
Sunning by a stream, a blue-yellow something that bore
The luring burnish of unfamiliarity:

He pointed, Schrock swung, missed (though he stood nearer),
And out went Russel's net—bagged it, to be sure,
But bagged *what*?
        A nothing . . .
              Could it be?
Yes a nothing: a nonesuch: a no-known-category::
Yes a creature nurtured outside the literature,
Never heretofore fixed in the mirror
Of language, the frame of measurement;
Yes oh please pray yes: yes to this heaven-sent,
Improbable but palpable singularity:
Please, praise the Lord: a new species:: oh, *glory!*

And when school reopened in the fall
A changed man strode its hallways, one
Who now was *news:* there was an article about
Their expedition and discovery in *The Blaze,*
The school paper . . . A changed man: slow
To grow but resolute, not reaching his full
Height till this his twenty-first year—just a hair below
Six feet, a bit gangly, still too thin, but
Burnt and bleached and rugged-looking with his days
Of combing the hills under a Rocky Mountain sun.

And a second appearance in *The Blaze,*
This time as one of Six Who Will Make a Difference.
    The upshot was that the now-lanky little boy
From Storey, who was always launched on some
Pressing errand; who had no truck with class politics;
Who seemed convinced all days were workdays;
Who stirred a sort of proud but edgy deference
Among the professors; and who was rumored to come
From substantial money—now began to enjoy
One of the benefits of being a "big wheel": sidekicks.

They came at him singly, shyly, one tattered
And woebegone misfit after another,
Hungerers after secrets, praise, encouragement, hope—
Orphaned souls seeking some kind of soul brother.
And Russ didn't begin to know how to cope
With their mute cries for attention, for affection,
For a philosophy suitable to lead
Men utterly lacking all sense of direction . . .
Like his father, Russ felt an instinctive need
To keep the world distanced, even as he felt flattered.

In truth he savored the sound of that inner voice
Declaring, with all the matter-of-fact confidence
Of a good reporter, *There goes one of those*
Six Who Will Make a Difference, even if, hurrying
For the lab, he has no time to grant the boys
More interviews today—relished the notion
That by a careful accounting of the rows
Of scales configuring a fritillary's wing,
Or by exposing chitin to close examination,
A man could, yes, make a difference.

Just so *heartening,* this intimation
That the pursuit of the minute is no cul-de-sac:
That you go way down deep, funneling your mind
Into the chamber of a waterdrop, through the fun-
house mirrors of a microscope, and when you loop back,
Step back blinking into the sun
Once more, what are you likely to find?
A world eager to engage and befriend you,
A world freshly arranging to send you
Acknowledgments, acclaim, another invitation . . .

One of which, in February of '09,
His junior year, includes an afternoon
Dance at Luetter House (Loot House) . . . Well, Russ
Heretofore has made it something of a policy
To avoid dances as doubly hazardous—
Combining, as they do, an abundance
Of young ladies with a prime opportunity
For revealing one's own clumsiness;
Yet now he hears a voice within announce, *I guess
I'll do it:* yes, Russ Darlington will attend the dance.

Dances? Breeding grounds for queer happenings, but all
Of them eclipsed when something comes to pass
That falls little short of a miracle:
This moment when a classmate shuffles forth to confide
That Pauline Beaudette (by common consent, the pride
And reigning beauty of the junior class),
Would not disdain, indeed might welcome, an advance
From Russ . . . *Hmm? What? Pauline?* Yeah. No
Kidding. *You're sure?* And the reply: Ask her. Go
Ahead, Russ. Ask Pauline to dance.

A dare which our Russ, with a courage he wasn't sure
He was in possession of, steps forward to meet.
     Pauline? he mumbles humbly, she scrutinizes
Her dance card; yes, it seems he—appears she might let—
Yes evidently Russ will have his dance . . . He steps away
Amazed, as he only now realizes
The scariest task still lies before him: hey,
This Storey boy who was born with two left feet
Must now, somehow, step out upon a dance floor
With none other than—Pauline Beaudette!

Her sort of beauty's the sort which, at close range,
Turns all but blinding; before a dance with her, a man
Might logically retreat into a stall
In the gentlemen's lavatory where he can
Freely strike the side of his skull with his fist
To render such good fortune plausible.
Yes, everything's come true, and nothing's so strange
As this way that miracles steadily come to light;
Nothing is so strange, and yet so right,
As his leading her to the dance floor by the wrist.

Leading *her,* in her blue dress, Pauline, round and round,
Inhaling in her presence a scent he cannot name,
Deeper than any words.
                              Man is endowed
With more scent-glands than any other primate,
And the angels doubtless possess more of them still:
Richer perfumes, heaven's censers . . . Hers is a blue flame
That reaches for the sky (as fire will),
While the two of them make for higher ground:
This the closest he's come to walking on a cloud,
Or call it a new evolutionary state.

Yet when the music slips out from under their dance
She nods, thanks him, *pins* him with her smile,
And walks off—gone, as if some doubt remained
That their lives had been transformed. Meanwhile,
As the backward-looking weeks pass, what can't be doubted
Is that somehow the spectacle of Pauline and Russ
Out on the dance floor—intertwined, self-contained—
Has been clarifying, anyway, for various
Female minds, not all of his former acquaintance;
Something has happened, his life has been rerouted,

He encounters women wherever he goes:
Girls who need help with directions, with corrections,
Who do not understand the professor's instructions,
Those whose books tumble to the floor just when he
Happens to pass by, those who wish merely
To say they admire the work he does . . . Could this be
What it would be to be a *ladies' man*? Heaven knows
It's a charming existence, and yet
Can only come to nothing in the end, clearly,
Since his heart must belong to Miss Beaudette.

—Who, to his dismay, never manages quite to be
Within reach of private conversation.
—Who, to his puzzlement, seems unaware
Of any business between them left unattended.
—Who, to his chagrin, seems to travel everywhere
Within a sort of military formation,
A phalanx of young men, from whose well-defended
Center she shoots him a friendly yet a vacant glance,
Till he almost has to wonder whether he
Invented the whole thing—their perfect dance?

Oh it's mid-May before he chances to flush
His quarry on the Quad—who bestows on him so warm,
So rich a smile, no one could ever gainsay
Her hand once lay in his, her waist within his arm.
Oh *Pauline* . . . Words long to tumble, all in a rush,
But where to begin? He doesn't know—
And summer coming—what if they'd both gone away
Without this moment? He explains that he'll be
Heading "way out west," to New Mexico,
Hunting butterflies—then home, to Storey. And she?

Well, back to St. Louis (which she calls Saint Louee,
As a little joke) and her army of aunts
(Most of them deaf, half of them blind),
And oh, how she envies him this chance
To go where he wants, to explore, to be—free!
   Well it's great, sure—but would she do him the favor—
Would she, if he were to—well, would she mind,
Would she answer, that is, if he wrote her a letter?
   Oh, that would be a godsend, Russ! A real lifesaver!
Nothing—she would like *nothing* better . . .

Across the empty, echoing, grandcanyonlike expanse
Of that summer, Russ addresses five letters to
St. Louis, none of which manages to spark
The faintest smoke signal of a response,
This being but one of his summer's two stark
Setbacks, the other his failure to gather
A new species—whose name would reflect his *own* ties
And loyalties. (Last time, Schrock, as his simple due,
Seized this perquisite of the insect's "author,"
Though neither spotter nor catcher of last summer's prize.)

September, Russ returns to school
To confront, face on, the death of every hope:
To hear how Miss Beaudette's officially taken—
Engaged to Patrick Pacey McCord, widely known
As one of the richest men on campus.
(PPMcC Sr.'s the "King of Bacon"
On the Chicago Exchange.) Russ, you fool
(He scolds himself), you're feeling lost without a compass?
Well then, boy, it's time to put your head down—
The only way, anyway, to meet a microscope.

Even so, he can't help being aware,
Catching Pauline's eye a couple of times,
Of something jittery/shy in the flashing looks
She fires his way—something maybe verging on despair?
Could it be she shares his yearning?
   Such thoughts aside, he's buried so deep in his books,
He's a month behind the rest of the world in learning
That Miss Beaudette has cut McCord
Long ago—time enough, indeed, to have secured
A brand-new fiancé, one Robbie Toombes.

... Toombes? Instantly clears her name of the vulgar gleam
Fixed to any girl rumored to be a gold-digger.
He's—well, quite a specimen, give him that:
Tall, with sea-blue eyes, and a jaw like a fist,
Someone who, even strolling the Quad, exudes the vigor
And the assurance and the rolling poise
Of the born athlete (he's captain of the baseball team).
In addition, he's a quick study (Dean's list).
And yet his father's a Gary factory rat.
Toombes? One of the scholarship boys.

But a new year brings blazing word of a new page
In the Pauline Beaudette Story. It would appear
She's buried Toombes as well, and on the Saturday
Morning when Russ, crossing the Quad, chances upon her,
She could hardly be friendlier. Or prettier.
(But that goes without saying.) It's one of those weird,
Chill, still winter mornings when every word
Emerges amplified and crystal clear,
As though the two of them stood upon a stage,
As though they were characters in a play.

He (with stammering urgency): How are you, Pauline?
She (smiling brightly): *Cold,* I s'pose. Refrigerated.
   But tell me (mock-solemnly), how are all the bugs?
He (treating the question gravely): Complicated.
She: Isn't everything? (But now the girl blinks, shrugs,
   And, looking away, finds a tone that instantly
   Evokes for them a new level of intimacy.)
   You're the expert: Is there, anywhere in Nature,
   Such a thing as a really simple creature?
He (hoping to match her gravity): Not that I've seen.

And if he'd dreamed of her for months, only now
Does it grow obvious just how
Desirable is this other soul, as a calm,
Grown-up melancholy suffuses Pauline's eyes:
A weighted look he longs to ease,
To share, to lighten . . . Russ feels outmatched,
Pulled two ways at once, this way and that
(Oh, his poor heart—that frantic little pit-a-pat!—
Just like a mouse curled shivering in your palm:
Nothing but a pulse beat with a tail attached).

It's this openness, this access of intimacy,
Inspires him to ask what he normally
Never would think to ask a woman he's drawn to:
"D'you want to see something of the work I do?"
Just so, in this linear fashion,
Beauty with beauty, passion with passion,
Are the dual strands of his life made one, in a scene
He'll not forget: Pauline Among the Butterflies
(Who are, it turns out, social insects, like ants or bees,
For today the butterflies meet their Queen).

Easy to dazzle her right off: show her a blazing
Cymathoe, for instance, one of the world's few
Truly *red* butterflies; or the eye-catching blue
Of a Morpho whose dun underside sports a row
Of big, free-floating, false eyes; or a Northern Jungle Queen,
Alit with dark diamonds; or the amazing
Labyrinth of a Mosaic's wing; or a Striped Blue Crow;
Or a Madagascan Sunset Moth, the iceberg green
Of its forewings melting into a smoldering
Tropical sunset at the tornus of each hind wing.

But the point—the point is subtlety. Perhaps begin
With a tiny Grizzled Skipper
Whose frail "fur coat" will see it through
The subarctic's sudden summer storms;
Or a little Atala, whose electric-blue
Spots on the coastal wings yield a shy, perfect grin,
So the creature becomes a floating smile, asail
Through seas of leaves; or an otherwise bland Swallowtail
Whose hind wing trailing exquisitely forms
A dancer's tapered leg, bound in a ballet slipper . . .

Finally he unveils the apotheosis
Of the collection, that brave little flash of gold
Which, last summer, the two "prospectors" culled
From a streambed: *Sulfuria bettina,*
Named for Schrock's mother. Of course the specimen
Might have borne another name—*Sulfuria paulina,*
Say. Until last year (he explains) this
Was a creature new to science, one
That Adam somehow, when he undertook
The naming of the animals, managed to overlook.

"There will be others," Russ continues. "Someday
I'll reach the jungle—" (*Jungle*: a word than which
No other sound, save *Pauline,* is half so rich.
Meanwhile, out the window, trees are denuded:
For this is Indiana in the dead
Of winter.) "—where whole genera of butterflies
Still go unnamed. So it will be up to me—"
In the lab's glassy, snowy light, she meets his eyes.
Was ever love pledged so surely? What more could a man say?
"—To fix their names for all eternity."

*

And now things happened very fast . . . Good golly
(A phrase he favors, playing up the hick),
Just two weeks later where does he wind up but
At a party seated beside her and what
Are they drinking? Sloe gin. And what are they doing?
Well, they're wearing party hats and blowing
Party favors . . . It's all a sort of joke,
Of course, or pair of jokes—a combination
Of some English aristocratic folly
And a child's birthday celebration—

This rubbing elbows with a crowd heretofore
Known only by rumor and hearsay:
The Dowsers Club, quite an exclusive set,
Wealthy boys renowned for working hard at play,
Partial to parties and dances, pranks
And parodies and carefree extravagances—
Generally not the sort to open a door
To Russ Darlington, here this evening thanks
To the powers of that queen of all dances
And extravagances, Pauline Beaudette.

"Russel, what in the world do you think
You're doing now?"
                           This from *her,* and what, in fact,
Is it he's doing? Good heavens—some partygoer
He turns out to be . . . He feels his face go pink.
After two gins (two being one more than enough,
Evidently), he's embarked on something *mortifying.*
What is he doing? Well—having put a party-blower
To his lips (one of those paper coils that puff
To a stiff cylinder when inflated, then retract
With a snap when the air goes out), he'd started trying

To get some inkling ... Well—just now, you see,
He realized this might be the closest he
Would ever come to putting himself in the place—
To understanding, that is, how it feels to be equipped
With a butterfly's proboscis and to draw
All nutriment through a collapsible straw;
To have, see, this elaborate *thing* on your face,
Sensitive and strong, this tool that might be slipped
Down the long throat of an orchid to seize
The treasure hidden in the nectaries ...

But what is he doing? Oh, dear Lord,
He's somebody who, invited to spend
An evening at the Dowsers Club—to mix
With the sharpest crowd imaginable—goes and sticks
A kid's toy in his mouth and starts to pretend
He's got the nose of an insect! *That's the sort of guy
He's always been,* or the life he was moving toward—
The freak he was destined to become—had he not met
The life-changing force embodied by
Beautiful, smart, and *savvy* Miss Beaudette.

What is he doing? He's having one more of those
Sloe gins! Ladies and gentlemen, he's getting set
To dance! And, tonight—tonight he's celebrating
His escape from the sort of behavior
That turns a man into a freak in the world's eyes,
A bug-chasing freak, laughed at wherever he goes.
   Tonight he's saying his final goodbyes
To the ludicrous disaster-in-waiting
That was Russel Darlington before Pauline Beaudette.
Rescued! Oh my most precious girl. My savior . . .

Later, in his gratitude, and in his keen sense
Of triumph (and in, perhaps, the ebullience
Of a first triumphal meeting with sloe gin),
He finds the raw courage to embrace
The girl. Eyes half shut, he wades right in,
Proceeding less by sight than touch; grips
Her upper arms in his hands; and dares to place,
Not once but twice, his lips upon her lips.
(And there just might have been a third
Such kiss, had he not, the second time, discovered

That in the single-minded, pellmell
Rush of the embrace he'd got his right arm pinned
Between his shoulder and hers, with his fingers
Clumped at the bare, moist, warm-skinned
Base of her throat, wrist jammed up against the satin swell
Of her breast. This
               is a new music and a new dance—
Pulse beat laid on heartbeat—whose rhythm lifts, and lingers,
Oh my angel girl!)
               (He'd have pulled away, of course,
Had his angel not, in answering his advance,
Clung to him with a wrestler's force.)

   And here's the question to be debated
Thousands of times in the months ahead:
Did she know? Was this particular contact knowing
Or unknowing? In either case, again that inner
Warmth of hers, like some thermal spring upflowing
From the very depths of her torso, a call
For which (it seemed) his own body had preformulated
Answers. Unknowing? Knowing? If the former, then all
His speculations were far worse than misled,
They were an affront to her honor;

But if the latter, the truth was—well, he wasn't one
To censure her. No, what he would have her know
Is that he was no prude—to know that he,
In matters sexual, was no innocent. Although
She was, true enough, the only girl he'd ever kissed,
Still he had thought hard about the topic, yes he'd
Subjected this business of sex to a scrutiny
Few men of his age, surely, had ever focused
Upon it. Just how many of his classmates had
Pondered Darwin so deeply as he'd done?

Who else understood so well the process of mating?
Was aware, e.g., that the male flea's complex sex ex-
tends half his body length? Or knew that males
Of some bee species will explode their genitals
On the queen? Or had heard of the hanging flies' sex-
For-goods exchange—a bribe of fresh-killed prey—
The Mrs. dining leisurely as the Mr. has his way?
Who else knew that if you decapitate
A male mantis (head torn right off by its mate)
He will not only go on copulating

But perform all the better for the lack of a brain?
How many had examined (as Russ had, carefully)
The tools of the trade—tools fit for the dark domain
Of the dungeon and the torture chamber? Here was love
Equipped with barbed members for facilitating rape,
With glue and fetters; here was a male realm of rip
And puncture, of plug and sperm shovel, club and lance,
And a female world of partners eaten alive . . .
(Compared to which Pauline's "tricks"—her daring glance,
Her close-fit dancing—were demure as demure could be.)

It's all about signaling, of course—the antic
Blue of the booby's foot; the lacewing's knock;
Deep in the reeds, the lowdown bullfrog's steady
Present, present, even at the risk that the call
Will materialize not a mate but an owl;
The coded fireflies' cool-burning *Ready, ready;*
The trailing plumes of the angelfish and the peacock;
The peacock moth putting into flight
The chemical lure that will pilot frantic
Fluttery males through miles of blackest night.

Theoretically, it's possible to live, die,
And afterwards lapse into one's constituent core
Elements without first passing through someone's di-
gestive tract (incinerated by fire, say), and yet
The percentage of lives that actually do so
Is negligible. No, your fate is sealed *ab ovo:*
In time to be laid out as somebody's omelet.
Eat *and* be eaten. Life's sole, limited winner?
The one who succeeds in reproducing before
Becoming somebody else's dinner.

Signals? So too was Pauline's hair's perfume,
And the perhaps subtly enhanced redness of her lips;
So too her eyelids' flutter and the upstart bloom
Of her breasts; so too the feel against his fingertips
Of her firm warm arm and her body's pledge of a shared
Internal *heat:* all forms of speech, extended
Metaphors in some root-language which
Predated words. The true mother-tongue is mute. And rich
Beyond all paraphrase. So he was hardly prepared
To censure her, if the contact was intended.

But if an accident—*if* she were blameless?
(The debate went on and on.) How would Pauline feel
To know he'd likened her, in the High Court
Of his mind, to a moth, a vixen, a pigeon,
And heard echoes in her laughter of a monkey's bark?
   Wouldn't she be shocked to learn just how shameless
He was, at bottom? And Russ in bed felt, at the thought
Of his thoughts, the blood like a creeping army steal
Over his face—his blush itself but one
More signal, this one lost to the dark.

(*You know you're a true entomologist*
If—if on those infrequent but
Not-rare-either occasions when your fingers climb
Down past the sealed door of your navel to form a fist
Around their brother-limb, you find yourself wondering
Suddenly, with dizzying fervor, exactly what
It would be like, like the dragonfly,
To mate and—over riffled streams, over thundering
Flumes, over lily-pad–paved ponds, over high
Seas of silky corn—to fly at the same time.)

He longs to be forgiven—and longs to tell her there's
Nothing for him to forgive. He wants to explain
That he approves of that buried heat she bears,
Which is no less than Life itself . . . The girl is *Life,*
Gentlemen, and isn't it Life we're here to celebrate?—
This the quality a man will instinctively seek
As he ventures off in search of a wife?
He wishes there were some way for him to speak
The various thoughts he has—tell it to her straight.
He wishes, in the dark, dawn would break upon the pane.

*

They didn't become engaged until
March the twenty-first—first day of spring
(A natural start for a naturalist),
With the wedding set for the nineteenth of June
(As near the summer solstice as possible).
John, on one of his swings through Old U,
Met his son's intended and, though his words were lost
In smoke, acceded.
          Much to be done, of course, and soon,
Starting with a suitable engagement ring,
And here again John Darlington came through.

It seemed there was a stone, rather sizable,
Belonging to Kathy, his wife, and if the two
Young people were of a mind—he'd like, not merely on
His own behalf, but Kathy's—Mrs. Darlington's—too,
Who he knew would share—would share his joy
In seeing her boy, her now-grown—
                                        But John
Couldn't quite finish. Meanwhile, Kathy's "boy"
Swelled with pride. The stone? Oh Russel knew
That stone, locked in John's desk some twenty years now:
Its white flame buried but unquenchable . . .

Having worried, for so many years, about
The *boy's* worrying (forever fretting that his son
Looked burdened—poor pale six-year-old swamp-ghost,
Poor pale ten-year-old with a college biology
Textbook in his lap), it pleased John to have most
Of the worries and burdens now descend upon
His own shoulders; pleased him to see
Russ impersonating a young man without
A care in the world, suddenly. Meanwhile, three
Unresolved issues were troubling John.

There was, first, the bride's vigorous campaign
On behalf of a Paris honeymoon, which,
Though strictly affordable, did not seem
Advisable. After all, there were certain fetters
Attached to a professor's salary;
This was no life of oysters and champagne.
Russ must consider his colleagues—mustn't play the rich
New boy in town among his elders and betters.
(In the girl's defense, France was an ancestral dream,
The Beaudettes having come from Tours originally.)

But any consideration of ancestry
Raised Worry #2. On learning of his son's
Engagement, John had bundled off at once
To St. Louis, for a look at the future in-laws.
It hadn't troubled him, much, to realize
The Beaudettes lived rather more modestly
Than Pauline might have led him to suppose.
(There was no sin in being poor, Lord knows,
Just as there was no virtue in mere wealth.)
No, the problem was simply a matter of health—

Or so the Beaudettes would have him believe.
But what did it mean that in the long weekend
Of John's stay the girl's mother was able to receive
Her visitor but once, briefly. She was "on the mend,"
He was told—though from *what* remained a mystery.
(The entire family breathed, somehow, an air
Of artful vagueness. Unsure what to think,
He half-suspected, given his own history—
Which drove him to see hidden spirits everywhere—
That Mrs. Beaudette's problem might be drink.

And third, there was—was what he chose to call
Pauline's *brightness* . . . a teasing ease and eagerness
That bookish Russel—earnest, out of step—
Could hardly follow. Would it be unjust
To call her a *coquette?* (In any case, not at all
The wife you'd picture for an entomologist!)
Flirtation was so much her way, she didn't stop
Even with *him*—batting her lashes, yes,
At her father-in-law-to-be! How was Russ
Ever to cope with such a one? It made John *nervous* . . .

Still, there was no disputing how *cheered*
The boy looked, with some much-needed
Color to his cheeks, tempering the blue blaze
Of his eyes and for the first time allowing John
To see just what a handsome son he'd reared.
In addition, it seemed Russ had hit upon
A new style of discourse—a frank and forthright
Strength in his gaze. Could it be that despite
His motherless upbringing Russ had succeeded
In finding a star to guide him the rest of his days?

John, as the day approached, did the new couple two
Further services . . . Having already supplied the girl
With the diamond for her engagement ring,
He lifted open the jewelry box once again
And fished out what Kathy once called her "finest thing"
(A choker of dark rubies, set off by a huge pearl).
This piece had lain on no neck but hers, and though
It seemed a cruel and somehow unexpected blow
To be asked to give it up, what choice was there, when
It was exactly what Kathy would have him do?

Next, on the very eve of the wedding, John took
His son to dinner at the Pfeiffer Hotel
In St. Louis and gave the boy a talk.
　　This was, of all paternal duties, the one he'd ask
To be excused from if he could, for who was he to give
Some other fellow words by which to live—
Who was he to *talk?* Yet Duty seemed to compel
John now to pose as an authority
On how a man should face the awesome task
Of securing a home for wife and family.

And so, all but forgetting even to sample
His splendid dinner, tamping his pipe, John spoke
Of Honor's role in any household—and the need
To keep what was most delicate alive—to heed
Unspoken feminine wishes—set an example
Not by word but deed—spurn the danger of male
Selfishness . . . Of course he couldn't begin
To say all he wanted to say. (At one point in the meal,
Relighting his pipe, he actually began to choke,
Like some sort of novice smoker.) He must start again.

He says: "Russ, do you know who's the most fortunate
Man in the world? The one slated to marry
His true love on the morrow." Only, John does not
Get as far as *morrow*. On the word *true*
The roots of his eyes begin to burn,
Tears boil over, his voice can no longer carry
The weight: out comes a high-pitched sob—

                                    And through

His tears he sees (sees, and instantly longs to die)
Sees he's scared the boy, who since the day he was born
Never once was asked to watch his father cry . . .

Sees Russel half risen from his chair, as though—
What? To help him? To make some show
Of soothing him, right here in the Pfeiffer Hotel?
Take his father like a baby in his arms? *Oh Jesus!*
John waves the boy back into his seat
And, rising himself, makes a quick retreat,
Lunging toward a men's room stall . . .

                              Oh no, *oh hell,*
Hasn't he outdone himself this time? Gone to pieces
So everyone can see?

                       Yes, that loud sob echoes,
Echoes infernally in his ears, even as he knows

This is one shame he will never shake.
And though it's years since he took a drink,
That night, hunched over the desk in his room,
He tosses back a bottle of bourbon "homegrown"—
(Bought for a dollar from a bellboy and yes
It's clear he *has* no shame, he's no better than some snake-
Oil salesman, he's no fit father of the groom).
Finding in its raw resinous stink
A welcome confirmation of his own
Wiggling and contemptible unworthiness—

And wakes the next morning to a howl
In the blood, shame a poison in each vein,
Head like a frying pan beaten with a spoon . . .
Shaves with shaky hands, gashes the wing of his nose,
Bloodies his own undershirt rather than impose
Himself unfairly on a hotel towel . . .
Off to church, where the glimpsed bride, white as the moon,
Fair as a rose, hits him like a nail to the brain.
Oh, she's much too fair, too pure to look upon.
Lower your gaze. Keep your head down, John.

THE JUNGLE

(1911–1912)

Nothing so definite as failure: no, not
As settled or as open as that, yet a sense
Within these new connubial arrangements
Of something oppressive, or suppressed,
Of daily shouldering a burden and finding
At day's end that the burden is your own life.
Not such an easy process, this binding
Of the threads (threads that can weave a hangman's knot),
This business of being man and wife.
Problems, problems in the nest . . .

Problems? In his mind he files, compiles, codifies . . .
There is
        1) the voyage he has so long planned,
His first real field-work, an ambitious
Nine-month expedition off to the land
Of, arguably, the world's finest butterflies:
Malaya. In a topsy-turvy realm where fishes
Climb trees, birds sleep upside-down, worms sing for rainfall,
Who is to say he will not discover the rarest,
The largest, the strangest, or simply the fairest—
The most beautiful butterfly of them all?

But Pauline wants him to postpone the trip.
The jungle? Alone? Russ, wouldn't it be more fun
If the two of us hopped off to the Continent—
London, Paris, Rome?
                     (Europe? Never having been there,
How can he explain just how feeble the grip
It has on his psyche? The most gorgeous European
Vista he's ever seen was a painting of Florentine
Rooftops, reds, browns, golds, an artful arrangement
Spun through the meditative glaze-glare
Of a tawny late-afternoon Tuscan sun—

Yet if it's exquisite mosaics for which
The heart hungers, the pantiles of Florence clearly
Fall short of the red-gold scales on a Marsh Satyr's wing
Bathed in the exclusive, private sun
Of microscopy's charmed circle: not merely
Richer hues than Italy's domes and towers
But richer history, winging back to the burgeoning
Cycads and horsetail ferns of the Triassic, when
The ur-lepidoptera first fluttered toward the niche
Reserved for airborne gems that live on flowers.)

To anyone who's managed an escape from Man's
Inherent partialities of scale
(The human assumption that large things
Are somehow grander than small), isn't it clear
That the Monarch's migratory cruise outspans
Magellan's, that the canals of Venice pale
Beside the venation of a damselfly's wings,
That the Black Forest could be tucked into the fur
Groves of a black witch moth? And Big Ben
Dwarfed by the hourglass on a black widow's abdomen?

There is
      2) the problem of the nonappearing soul,
The "blessed event" that has failed, so far,
To eventuate. At first, what Pauline had hoped for
Was to give him an heir before he set sail
For Malaya, but their dream met a delay,
And the revised hope was that as Russ
Embarked for the jungly ends of the earth
A second sea-journey would have begun—a solo
Sailor bound for that most miraculous
Of landfalls: the bourne of birth.

But no: month after month instead
A silent, sullen flow of blood closeted
Behind the bathroom door—and all the blood
Gone from Pauline's face when she emerged to nod
Confirmation of his failure. His? Apparently,
Or so her look implied: as if to say that in all
His moments of passion, every heaving delivery
Of hundreds of millions of cells, still
Some falling short was palpable—some small
But essential balking of the will.

There is
          3) the fact that (and this one's the most
Astonishing of all) Pauline is "bored."
Bored? He scarcely knows what to say,
How to address a condition so queer,
He for whom there never are enough hours in a day.
But what is she to do? *Just what am I supposed
To do, Russ?*—she who has no hobbies, tends
To leave books unfinished, has always ignored
Her correspondence, and somehow failed (it now grows clear)
To convert being popular into making friends.

With her typical shrewdness (oh he's quick
To concede her superior penetration
In the domain of personal affairs;
Her harshest judgments have a way of coming true)
She lays it out more neatly than he'd be likely to:
"I'm not wild about the ladies, Russ—and you prefer
I avoid the fellas." He's prone to jealous fears,
True enough (the mere sight of her in conversation
With another man can set his blood astir,
And to watch her dance makes him faintly sick),

Yet there's something odd in her tone, even so,
When speaking of old girlfriends—a chilliness
Toward women generally. It's almost as though
All of them are suspect (which comes as news
To Russ, whose admittedly limited dealings
With young women have confirmed a long-held sense
Of their natural goodness and finer feelings).
Not even Pauline's mother is above
Such suspicions (indeed, if seldom spoken of,
Mrs. Beaudette inspires especial vehemence).

As for her old girlfriends, Pauline feared (so she confessed),
"They're all laughing at me"—words that strike
Russ to the heart, the more so since he can't contest
Suspicions he scarcely understood.
Was it chiefly her childlessness, or her marriage to
The "bug man," that rendered her ridiculous?
He takes to leaving the lab more often than he should,
Far more often than he would like,
Solely to sit with her and ponder this
Query he cannot answer: "So what should I do?"

He sits helpless and, at times, half blinded
By a powerful, paradoxical anger
Fueled by his own powerlessness. And sits wondering,
And frightened, on days when Pauline seems immersed—
Like someone underwater—in a languor
Thickening her every motion . . . And sits reminded
Of how he'd known from the start—the winter day he first
Showed her his butterflies—that this vexed creature's
Beauty was never so intense, more ravishing
Really, than when sorrow brushed her perfect features.

And there are
                4) stray hints of *something else,* lurking
At the root of his troubles, and extending well
Beyond and beneath the two of them: what's at stake
Dwarfs any pair of newlyweds and their
Minor domestic agitations:
                       a sense
Of nothing less than some diabolical force, working
Its ends upon the planet . . . For most temperaments
It seems the gradually surfacing nightmare
Generated in the *Beagle*'s wake
Is a vision of a ship with no one at the wheel:

The earth as a vessel sailing the centuries
Without a piloting hand (while, deep in the hold,
Its cargo multiplies, modifies, undergoes
Transmogrifications). But for Russ the miscreance
Runs deeper: the notion that Darwin's engine—
The errant juggernaut of Natural Selection—
Is *malign,* and as you close in on Nature, you close
On something far worse than indifference:
Pure evil. Evil spun into the shaggy trees
And the worm's strait corridors; evil in the leaf-mold;

Evil in the stalking kitten as it prods
A ball of twine, and in the tidy fox,
Licking clean the bowl of an egg; evil of the pink mouse,
Eyes still shut, and the spider's open house;
Evil in the white oval bomb of the sphex,
Strapped to the paralyzed spider, set to detonate
In a few days' time, when the emerging larvae eat
Their inert host alive; evil in all living things
Save those Olympians adrift on papery, glyph-coded wings—
Errant stationery
                of a race of benign gods.

Like others before him, Russ turns for rest
And relief to poetry: that meted, paced-off plot
Where nothing enters save by invitation.
His feeling for Wordsworth—could it be, from the soil
Of mere respect, sympathy, admiration,
Might now spring a fruit that would feed his soul?
In any event, he liked how Wordsworth addressed
The soul, with sureness yet concern, as of a plant,
An "exotic," brought from some faraway land—
Hardy, yet ill-suited for the conditions at hand.

For the man Wordsworth searched and found the Good,
Affirming equally the common clay,
The night sky's glitt'ring sweep, the brotherhood
Of man—who saw, in all he saw, the plans
Of Providence, at once writ large and "buried
In glory, far beyond the scope of man's
Enquiring gaze . . ." Yes, this was someone who
Felt certain "Nature never did betray
The heart that loved her" (a sentiment, it's true,
Composed by someone who had not yet married).

Like a leak in the cellar—the roundabout way
Resentment gathers . . . You bail with cup and pail, you
Make repairs to the masonry, still it will seep
Back into the house each night, even as you sleep;
And each day bringing nearer the day
Of Russ's departure.
                    Where is he headed? *Down,*
Below the equator, to a whole new hemisphere—
Leaving, meanwhile, his young wife here
Alone, in this small midwestern college town,
To contend with the question, *What am I to do?*

Each passing day resentment mounts,
Until eased, all at once, by the ingenuity
Of someone who's forever devising a plan
To lighten a loved one's load. It's John Darlington
Who proposes—John Darlington, the most thoughtful man
Who ever lived—that Pauline might "find it fun"
(Pitched in her language, no less) to accompany
His son as far as San Francisco, in which case he'd
Like to provide the train passage—indeed,
Already has looked to a few arrangements . . .

San Francisco! Pauline's out of her chair—rushes
Forward to seize her father-in-law's hands
(John nearly swallows his pipe—mumbles—blushes),
Then she's off across the room to seize
Her husband's hands (who blushes too). Ah, grace:
Recovered bliss, a happy home . . . Russ
Hardly knows what to say, but understands
From the expression on his father's face
He should say little. (John's look begs him, *Please,*
This will be easier if you make no fuss.)

Arrives a day, then, or a night, an occasion
To which repeatedly—over every
Broken decade until the end of Russ's life—
His thoughts will home, thousands of times
Reverting to this: two young lovers, man and wife,
Locked in a train car that huffs and sways and climbs
Into open, thin-aired terrain (the lovers, too,
Locked in a swaying passage through
A breathless land), slips and spills eventually
Over the living spine of an unrolling nation,

In darkness, as a curtained moon lights the snow
(A crippled man will naturally go back
To such things: sensations of large-scale
Motions in a small space, your every nerve
Installed in the womb for just this interdependency
Of warmth with warmth, curve with curve,
Even while the ongoing embrace of train and track—
A hurtling spark racing along an icy rail—
Strikes up its own clamorous affinity),
And the snow returns a lunar glow.

And arrives a day—to one who has waited
His whole life—when a young man from the Great Plains
Finds the cornfields and wheatfields of home translated
Into the largest of the Seven Seas.
The planet is luminous from one rounded rim
To the other. He has set sail. The Pacific contains
Volumes that bedazzle and finally benumb him.
(To ponder the total number of gallons bathed in sun
Is dizzying—to say nothing of, ton on ton,
The ebony depths, the ear-popping densities.)

The year is 1912, his homeland is receding . . .
Quite the best time, as a toy-size steamer inches
Across the Pacific, for a twenty-four-year-old
Naturalist to light out for those brave jungles where
A newer New World's waiting to unfold!—
Just a decade since an obscure Swiss monk, long dead,
Was resurrected from his seminary bed,
And now there's the promise in the air
(Everyone feels it!) of somehow feeding
Mendel's peas to Darwin's finches.

(Meanwhile, in Manhattan, this very year—
1912—in the "Fly Room" at Columbia U,
Thomas Hunt Morgan has begun to see the light
In *Drosophila melanogaster,*
Soon the "most famous insect in scientific history,"
The red-eyed fruit fly and the mutant white.
Battening on mashed banana, a new
Generation is bred and catalogued every
Ten days. Things are coming clear, moving faster;
A revolution's brewing in the atmosphere.)

He has a sense of himself as, one might say,
Precious cargo: of a lofty destiny
And this a scene of epochal moment, the *Return*
Transporting young scientist Russel Darlington
On the first leg of his voyage across the sea.
Who can predict what things he'll learn?
He knows, anyway, that everything he's ever done
Has pointed him toward this opportunity
To blaze a path which others in time will take;
Posterity itself is swirling in his wake.

—Precious cargo, yet perishable:
Anyone heading into the jungle must
Confront the possibility of peril
On all sides. Luckily, he gets advice he can trust
From a missionary he meets on the boat,
And while in Honolulu Russ puts up at
A Baptist boardinghouse ... The town's afloat
In vice and sin; there's no not noticing that.
But soon he'll be gone, and will be the happier
For having kept himself in all ways pure.

The expedition will begin in earnest when
He reaches the fabled Carolines
And the obscure, overgrown island of Ponape,
Where, in a sort of test run for the Malay,
He'll spend a few weeks, carve out a new regimen:
Hike, climb, collect a little data,
Maybe even learn to read a few of the signs
Of the jungle ... Small islands, it's true,
Are usually poor in butterflies, but who
Can say for sure? This is called *Terra Incognita*.

Darwin in the *Voyage* recounts an amazing sight
Miles off Patagonia: a cloud of butterflies
Stretched on and on beyond all reckoning,
So dense the sailors cried it was like snow . . .
And the thought of that cloud eternally asail
Upon a page of prose returns Russel to the rail
Of the *Return,* once more to survey the skies
And a tropical sun that overmasters *everything:*
Every cubic inch in the firmament aglow.
(There's more light in Heaven than he'd figured on, quite.)

Here are whole days in which, from dawn to dusk, a sun
Far too potent for this world holds dominion,
So that not even the most casual act is done—
No flying fish break for a moment from the blue,
No spider on the ship's rail haul its fly to bed,
No gull flutter down for a closer view
Of an ambiguous patch of sea-spray,
No floating coconut, like a shrunken head,
Turn the other cheek in the sea's chop and sway—
Save as a reflection of the sun.

Darwin weighs on Russ's imagination,
Naturally, who took as a vade mecum on
His circumnavigation of the globe a copy of
Paradise Lost, that tale of creation
Which Darwin himself was destined to undo
(Destined, like those errant rock-sheets that so preyed upon
His thinking—marine fossil-beds two miles above
The ocean, hundreds of miles from any coast—
To disturb, derange, recast,
And, ultimately, to create anew).

Only fitting, then, that Russ tote a book as well.
His choice is *The Prelude,* which, as day breaks from the sea
Each morning, he reads aloud on deck, reveling
In a misted, sheep-cropped Albion. But what would old
Wordsworth make of the raw metallurgy
Of tropic waters, the molten tin and beaten gold,
The sprinkled zinc, the copper in the sea breeze's bite?
Surely no poet, ever, got this right:
    Ocean forged by a blacksmith god, a hammering
    Sun, and the ringing core of the earth for anvil.

But Russ has difficulties with Darwin, even now.
A stubborn sympathy for the fallen rival
Leaves him feeling that evolution's co-
Discoverer, Alfred Russel Wallace, somehow
Met an unjust fate; through a heartless "survival
Of the fittest" (Spencer's phrase, actually),
One worthy pushed another into obscurity—
The final outrage of extinction. (It's almost as though
The theory, by burying a founding father,
Sought to extend its scope a little farther.)

(Resentment of Darwin will look absurd to Russ
In later years, who will grow to understand
With the slow-won clarity of the handicapped
The full extent of the great man's mysterious
Ailments—headaches, boils, nausea—which left him forever
Struggling up out of his invalid's bed
To pursue the few hours of work each day permitted.
An easy ride? Not for Darwin, back in England
To stay, nor for Wallace either, wrapped
In the cold, blanketing sweats of malarial fever;

Nor, for that matter, for Russ Darlington, who
Never quite made it out of the starting gate,
His abbreviated quest bringing him home again
To live, day in, day out, with chronic pain . . .
In time, Russ will see himself as humbly linked to these
Two colossi, with whom he shares (in addition to
An urge to override the merely physical)
A kinship of name-similarities:
Wallace's middle name is Russel, and the fall
From *Darwin* to *Darlington* is not so great.)

Cross a sea to cross the invisible boundary
Of a dateline—a phenomenon
Not much less odd and unearthly than alpenglow,
Or bead lightning, or a double rainbow.
Somehow the steamer's steady chugalug propels
You into tomorrow, like something in H. G. Wells,
Whose Time Traveller was "flung into futurity."
(Though as for that, his entire enterprise
Has its own motive logic—Russ has always known
His destiny lay under equatorial skies.)

Arrives a day when a cliff walls up out of the sea,
An immense basalt barbican, menacingly bare:
The holy height known as Sokeh's Rock. It's the end
Of the beginning, Russ has done it, reached Ponape,
Found his future in a spot that nobody
He knows has ever heard of; this is where
He'll enter the jungle *as an explorer*. Today,
Leaning on the ship's rail, he feels a salted blend
Of elation, vertigo, wonder, and fear
At this notion that the future's, finally, here.

But first, formalities . . . Time to explain his mission
To the German port officers who have stood
As gatekeepers to this island since it was bought
From Spain in '93. And here, to his surprise,
He's received rather coolly; you might say
They run a tight ship, ashore. He'd thought
His dutiful academic German would
Grease a few wheels—and yet the gray
Funktionär who interviews him, a Herr Preis,
Seems to regard him with suspicion.

Youthful exuberance nonetheless carries the day.
The uniformed Herr Preis warms to the thing
Eventually, says, "Butterflies, eh?"
(Of course for Preis they're *Schmetterlinge,*
A word completely lacking in *poetry* so far
As Russ is concerned. Compare
Mariposa or *myrtil* or *fjaril* or *vlinder*
Or the lovely, papery *papilio*.) Herr
Preis shifts to English suddenly: "I fear
You won't find much to interest you here"—

And yet, as though expressly to undo his denial
(As though to blazon the irrepressible
Fecundity of this most amazing isle),
At this very moment a blue-tailed skink appears
On the wall behind Herr Preis and, on legs faster
Than the eye can follow, veers
Into a rubbly hole in the plaster,
From which, wholly at rest, the creature peers
Mindfully, as though intending to
Record and assess this interview.

*

[And with this lizard scampering
Up the wall, I'd introduce myself at last: your guide
And interpreter, the overseer of the tale
Of Russel Darlington's long and ultimately
Stationary voyage—to which I'd hope to bring
A skink's skittery celerity
And untampering touch, its quick-eyed
Watchfulness and cool proclivity
For snug retreats, with the occasional urge to scale
The vertical, in defiance of gravity.

So much in the world is believable
Solely because it's real—like the migration
Of the Monarch, its brain the size of a bread crumb,
Annually managing to navigate from
Quebec to the Sierra Madres, a distance
Of two-thousand-plus miles . . . and while any invocation
To the Muse is apt, these days, to look too
Quaint to be credible, I'd turn for assistance
To the world's creatures: to cat, dog, sheep, hen, bull;
Kangaroo and kinkajou, gnu and kudu.

How was our Darlington to know that in just two
Years' time the Germans would be in flight
From Micronesia, refugees of a war
Bloodier than any the world had ever seen—displaced
By an invading Asian army preparing for
Still bloodier war? Or that his own path would be traced
By someone who dreamed of restoring the very light
Of his days—days of 1912—and the way it fell one
Morning on a brilliant young naturalist who,
Fresh from the Midwest, gaped at a tropical sun?

Hence a pilgrimage of my own, leading me,
In the summer of ninety-five (*nineteen* ninety-five,
Exactly one hundred years after this history
Springs open with a bullfrog's leap), to Ponape's
Jungles, hoping some trace of him might survive—
That in a green fabric that reweaves within days
Any rip or tear, I might somehow retrieve
Evidence of Russel Darlington. He had a call
That brought him here and so, so I would believe,
Do I: his—my—*Darlington's Fall.*

... A task that leads to an odd situation:
Having beached up on a tropical paradise,
I spend most of my hours indoors—long days
In the archives of the Jesuits, poring over
Old missionary records and letters, one by one,
The rare photograph, the odd customs declaration—
Out to achieve a near-miracle, to recover
Intact a thread laid on the floor
Of the jungle eighty-three years before:
The cord—the broken cord—of Russel Darlington.]

*

But while you're here (Herr Preis goes on) you must pay
A visit to the ruins of Nan Madol. Now *they*,
Truly, are *splendid*. Young man, in all the Pacific
You will find nothing, not even the monolithic
Heads of Easter Island, to equal them: ninety-three
Structures in total. Only a century ago
Ponape was home to an advanced society:
A true palace, with temples, markets, canals! Although
The natives have fallen into degradation since,
Know that this was the Venice of the Pacific, once.

—In this respect, Herr Preis misleads unwittingly,
Citing a recent archaeological survey
Soon to be debunked; it's been half a millennium
Since the collapse and abandonment of the Kingdom.
Otherwise, he misleads deliberately, giving a much-
Clipped account of last year's uprising—a mutiny
Of native workers not finally put down
Until seventeen rebels were led out at dawn
And dispatched by their German masters. Ponape
Is a powder keg, waiting for a match.

Accompanied by a German missionary
Born in, of all places, Hope, Pennsylvania,
Russ Darlington saunters the streets of Ponape's
One real town, the comically named Kolonia,
And marvels at so much he hadn't dreamed to find:
The shipyard and carpentry shop, the ruined maze
Of the old Spanish fort, the oil streetlamps, the tall
Coconut palms shading the cemetery
Where Spaniards and Germans lie, the roomy hospital
(No reason yet to pay it any special mind),

The flaking prison, the huge warehouse of the Japanese
Trading company (traffickers, it's said, in illegal
Arms to the natives), the spindly European fruit trees,
The police drilling-ground, the well-kept coastal road,
The competing Liebenzeller and Capuchin
Mission schools, where giggly, dark-eyed children are brought
Into the fold—Russel Darlington,
Age twenty-four, marvels at how much good's been wrought
In this remote site, under the black, white, and red
Emblem of the German imperial eagle.

And marvels, too, at how everything fixes
Itself, here at the ends of the earth, how simplified
Complex undertakings can be: you make a few
Inquiries, nod appreciatively, line
A couple of brown palms with a green dollar or two,
And wind up with a boat—an outrigger canoe—
That will take you to Nan Madol, and a guide,
The wonderfully named Immensio, who mixes
Un poco de English, a little Deutsch, eine kleine
Español . . . They'll do just *fine*.

But to call the ruins "splendid"?
                                    A laughable
Understatement. He's never seen their like before,
And perhaps they have no *like,* these colossal, steeple-
Sized basalt columns stacked log-cabin style
Upon each other: no calculating the tons of stone
In these typhoon-buffeted, overgrown,
Prone columns of a kingdom by the sea—
By a tropical sea whose cream-warm breakers pour
Over coral reefs and swampy greenery
To sift the ruins of a drowned people.

Neither a fluent nor a knowledgeable guide,
Immensio's all the more affecting
For the gaps he means to bridge with his wide-
Flung gestures; the man would conjure up immense
Dynasties—kings, priests, princesses, intrigues, cabals,
A cacophonous marketplace, palm-lined canals . . .
He speaks in a sort of soaring hush, reflecting
Both the grandeur of the dead and the deference
They demand of us even now. A race
Of titans once made this their dwelling-place.

Splendid? Well, if the word falls
Ridiculously short of Nan Madol's
Magnificence, it's far less adequate still
For the glories of Ponape's vegetation. Yes,
Darwin got the matter exactly right when,
After his first glimpse of jungle, in Brazil,
He wrote: "Delight itself is a weak term to express
These feelings . . . To a person fond of natural history,
Such a day brings a deeper pleasure than he
Can ever hope to experience again."

. . . Or nearly right, since Darwin evidently missed
What Russel intuits from the start:
The menace. If you could only strip away all
The lush krypsis, or learn to read the creepers' scrawl,
Follow the inmost path to the final twist
In the swamp, you'd come at last upon the oozing heart
Of something sinister . . . In all his keen
Appreciation, and awe, and of course delight,
He can almost ignore it, yet not quite:
Fear, revulsion—Russ, get out while you can.

His mute misgivings are corroborated by
The natives themselves, who—so he has read—
Regard the Interior with "superstitious dread."
(Local wisdom seems to be: hold to the shore,
Where danger is, at least, clear as the fin of a shark . . .)
Yet hugging the coast won't do for Russ. Fame
Lies inland. His task is to explore,
To pin down the specimens that he will name
To make his name. He must pierce the hadal dark
To fetch the bright Proserpina of a butterfly.

Part of his discomfort is his sensation, so
Starkly enhanced to the naturalist's eye,
That to enter jungle is to enter a war zone,
Leaf with leaf, and vine with tree: a green duel
To the death. Though the distinction he sees
Is illusory—though of course he's aware
That it's the same wherever you go, that any pair
Of lichens on an arctic scarp, themselves still as stone,
Are no less locked in combat than these—
He can't shake the sense that here the leaves are *cruel*.

But sometimes it does not do to brood too much.
Push on, he tells himself, push through.
With the Ponapean for butterfly, *lipahrourou*
(Fluttering Lady—isn't that fine?), and Immensio
As trusty guide, Russ takes keenly to trailblazing
Deep into jungle, threading pathways so
Tortuous, and so much alike, truly it's amazing
Any guide can keep them straight. And the butterflies?
—Scarce, in truth, but what can you expect under such
Overcast and rain-threatening skies?

Patience. The sky will clear. Meanwhile, pass the night
In the thatched huts of some cousins of Immensio's,
High on a mountainside. Where rooms have no walls,
Plants are your constant neighbors; Russ is aware,
In the dark, as they dine on breadfruit and sticky balls
Of rice, of another, wider circle of sound—
Leafy, digestive sighs and rustles. He feels a knot
In his stomach and boldly steps out for some air,
Into a black clearing that must be a garden: rows
Of modest vegetables, low to the ground.

Skies will clear. Darlington steps forth into a night
Of stars, shuffles into the magic oval of his high
Tropical garden, and feels the very dome
Of the heavens brought almost within reach:
Tonight, the sky invites the least stardust radiance
The way a pond will beckon to the swaying dance
Of a lantern; or a Saxon shield call to the light
From its dusty museum case; or a pearl come
Alive to a candle, cupping the flame in the rich
Curves of its luminous laminae . . .

The solitary man, come to astonish
Himself, he's the lank foreigner in the night-
Clearing, head back in awe at the multiplicity
Of the heavens. Darlington's come to the rim
Of the bulging equator, and from the height
Of his jungle clearing he can peer
Over the Line to the lights of a new hemisphere,
Looking over—across, down, above—
Toward a whole new bestiary: the Wolf, the Dove,
The Scorpion, the Centaur, the Flying Fish.

Stars without number, stars like the wing-blown
Blizzard beheld by the *Beagle*'s crew—
Or like those minuscule dots of sand in the blue
Map of the Pacific, scarcely visible,
Yet each potentially a home to unknown
Fauna, each island its own hot crucible
Of creation, stamping out its own
Butterfly species . . . and each species a solitary
Scale on the great wing of that visionary
Überseele, the Lepidoptera.

Never quite like this before: never the full-flung
Vistas of Heaven, and with them, more astounding still,
Inklings of his own place in their designs . . .
The year is 1912 and Russel Darlington stands
On the isle of Ponape in the Carolines,
One of two thousand islands in Micronesia, one among
Twenty-five thousand islands in the Pacific, and feels
As though he could cup the stars in his hands.
    His brain has cleared, his imagination reels,
And if the butterflies on this particular hill

Prove disappointing, he'll push farther into the wild:
New hills, new islands, chase the stars to even
Odder constellations, new configurations of palpi
And proboscis, thorax and valvae;
The whole of his life has guided him to this lost
Island that nobody he knows knows ... The child
Is father of the man, who reaches his final instar
Only in the jungle, far from everyone, far
From everything but the eyes of heaven,
Where he molts a final time, into manhood at last.

*

Daybreak. The night of heavy sleepers spins
An additional, plush, multi ply web, veil
Overlapping veil until the trees, the hill, the heavens pale
Into nothingness. Fog. Mist. *It go away,*
Immensio declares, which turns out to be true,
Though in piecemeal fashion: the fog thins
Reluctantly, in scraps and tatters,
Leaving, in a new blaze of green and blue,
Old, cobwebby pockets of gray—
Which, soon, the firm boot of the sun shatters.

A breakfast of tinned beef and rice is followed by
Lengthy debate between Immensio and various
Voluble cousins in which many *lipahrourous* fly—
Presumably an analysis of where
Fluttering Ladies are best pursued.
In the end it's decided that most of their
(I.e., Russ's) gear will remain here. They mean
To travel light, Immensio and Russ,
With little more than a net, a canteen,
Some specimen envelopes, a little food.

Morning sun coaxes out a real menagerie:
A couple of sulphurs (bagged) and what may be
A swallowtail (too distant for a swipe with the net),
A green dove, a reddish-brown parakeet, a big
Red-and-black dragonfly, a small brown bat,
Black bulldog ants, more blue-tailed skinks, a rheumy pig,
A weighty toxin-laden toad, a mad-eyed cat—
While, simultaneously, the heat and the sweat
Release sundry phantoms from under his lids:
The jungle's darker pockets are lined with shades.

Immensio cups a hand to his ear and grins: *Can*
You hear? Not initially, no, too dim,
Or the blood's too hard at his temples, but then
Russ makes it out, yes, a somehow wetter whisper than
Breeze-brushed leaves—the softest sound
Conceivable, the way a doting momma might call
A napping infant back into the sunlight, when
She isn't sure whether or not to awaken him—
Somewhere far above, all but lost, the round
Overarching *hush* of a waterfall.

And now the path turns trickier—up
A trickling streambed, dripping rock-faces
And pooled ditches, slimed roots, moss-seamed crevices.
And up, footholds the size of a teacup,
It's hard work, everything—everywhere—wet
Right through, ten minutes, twenty,
Sweat all the way down to your fingertips, sweat
Biting at your eyes. It's hard work: steep
And slippery perches, with plenty
Of chances for a spectacular misstep.

Go slow, Russ, one stepping-stone at a time,
Keep your eyes open, even as the sweat
Stings them shut, your hands serial and secure
In the slip and the wet, heart firm in the climb
Toward a wheeling whisper, the high plunging ledge
Of the falls . . . He's among boulders, safely set,
When he feels a sidelong pull, out at the edge
Of his vision, swings round and yes it's true:
In the shade, a detonating flash of blue,
A *fluttering lady,* blur of pure

Iridescence, like a morpho's . . . And it comes as a shock
(There are no morphos on Ponape), no, *this can't be*—
And all such a rush: he's *found* it, yes, a genuine
Discovery, maybe, and immediately
The hand hungers so much it makes your head spin,
And while you're bringing the net around
The other hand's spinning forward to seize
The anchor of a root, or a rock,
When something—root, rock—gives way . . . The ground
Shifts beneath him and all at once he's

Fixed at an impossible angle
And no means of support, he's a soul holding a root
Rooted to nothing, twisting and sliding back,

                                 his boot
Skidding on stone (and all so much faster than anyone can
Follow—all only later recalled or reconstructed):
The net slips in his hands, his body swings
Back, out on his back, as if the air might be trusted
To uphold him,

                as though he had wings—
Like a butterfly or an angel,
A moment falling

                blind, no angel-man but a man,

Head spinning, arms spinning, and then:
Crisp blows of lightning, inner splinterings
& the bright exploding blindness,

                      and maybe a call
Pushed out into the breathless intervals between
The leaves, or maybe within you instead,
No voices anywhere except in your head,
   Where dawns a realization of having been
Abandoned, a torso stripped of its wings,
Or arms, lost in leaves, the good guide gone, you're all
Alone, nothing but

                a rip in the green

Fabric, Russ,
        the rip already nearly mended . . .
There's a man underneath the curved hush of the falls.
(The falls—forever—go on reinventing the wheel.)
   And the romantic tale is abruptly ended
Of a young man who voyaged to tropical lands
In the name of science, scaled hills with hungry hands
(A treasure-hunter out for living jewels), found the high
Heights and fell,
        broken on the forest floor, left to die.
He's deep in the green. *Help me,* somebody calls.
Ghosts are airing rumors and the leaves have found their meal.

Home Forever

(1912–1916)

Afterwards he could never separate
The bark and bedrock of memory
From the runny clouds of fantasy,
Could never, no matter how hard
He tugged, yank loose the stark white root
Of certitude: everything blurred . . .
In his mind he kept going back, seeking the place where,
Underneath the pain and shock, under the furred
Filamented growths of nightmare,
The truth lay, clean and dry and scarred,

Yet he could never divorce what he recalled
From what was confected out of hearsay
And delusion.
                    It seems, notwithstanding
The many tricks his memory might play,
Immensio *hadn't* abandoned him after the fall,
He'd gone for help instead; that Russ had been hauled
Downhill by a team of men (only the Lord knew
At what cost to his spine), loaded onto a canoe,
Shipped up the coast—eventually landing
Back in Kolonia and the German hospital.

A German doctor treated him, assisted
By a nun from Strasbourg. Drugged, he slipped rapidly
Into fever, in the midst of which the good
Sister inquired (in German, or French, or English)
Whether he was Catholic or Protestant,
And Russel replied, with great dignity,
"I am a child of God"—or that's what he truly meant
To say. For he was so furious—or fearful—or feverish—
He may have said, instead, "I am no child of God."
No saying what he'd said; things were so misted.

Then fever coming down like the rain,
The two hundred inches of which per annum
Fall on Kolonia, rattling the tin
Roofs so lordfully no other talk's possible,
Then dropping to a whisper on a man immobile
In the heat and damp (confinement's internal in-
ferno), and more rain, blasting the tin tympanum,
And fever's bless'd return, when you first learn to pray
For delirium, for a dream from which you'll someday
Wake differently, if you wake again . . .

And yet Hell has its own way of clearing the smoke
While stoking the fire. His life's full horror
Wasn't manifest until, cast in plaster, he woke
Supine on a ship bound for San Francisco—
Stretched flat all day under a low lizard-green ceiling,
Its paint ripped by fever-blisters, and what
Was there for him to do, who couldn't move, but wait
For those paint chips to drop?—feeling
Less like a man than a piece of cargo,
To be labeled: Russel Darlington, Ex-explorer.

(Throughout the voyage, one image—one barbarism—
Sits like a weight on his chest, *in* his chest: somewhere
He'd read of giant tortoises, hauled
By the dozen off the dry hills of the Galapagos,
Stacked upside-down in a ship's hold.
Unable to *right* themselves, pawing the air
For some purchase, they had nothing to do but gaze
Into the dark, their capsized lives a long wait
To be eaten . . . From this image Russ would date
His eventual conversion to vegetarianism.)

A new old New World . . . In San Francisco he's met by
A delegation—his father, and Pauline, and a team
Of doctors—and meets up with heaps of scrambled eggs,
Sourdough biscuits, honey oozing from the comb,
Crisp bacon, steaming coffee and rich cream,
Fudge, wedges of gingerbread, warm apple pie . . .
There are tests, and one consultation
After another, and men to carry a man whose legs
Won't carry him, and at last a determination:
He is—the three of them are—heading home.

And so it happens that this body of his
That will scarcely move of its own
Locomotion, having been hoisted through
Jungle on the backs of natives, shipped by canoe,
Borne by steamer, by stretcher, and by motorcar,
Now rolls thousands of miles by train, all to place him
Where he originated: he has gone so far
As to wind up at home. How simple it is:
The story ends in Storey. We embark for the Unknown
And wind up in Childhood, frozen in time, in limb.

The body's packed in plaster, his head's a war-
Zone of pain and painkillers, one week
Bleeds into the next, with a dim sense, all the while,
Of his father's arranging things . . . Strange doctors come
(At what expense?) all the way from Baltimore,
Chicago, Cleveland, and their common conclusion
Is that Russ is one lucky man: his condition—
A ruptured lumbar disk (L3–L4), with some
Tearing of the spinal cord itself—might well
Have resulted in paraplegia. He will walk.

And one day John announces (gently,
Almost as if asking Russ's permission)
That he's found a big house in Remington, near
The University, and was wondering if—
Just a thought, Russ—this is assuming we're
All of a mind, you see—we might move this fall—
Easier for you there, to resume your work in full . . .
(And John Darlington? He means, evidently,
To pick up and depart without fuss or commotion
From the one town he's called home his whole life.)

But not even John Darlington can settle
The problem when a woman like Pauline winds up
Married to a cripple. Not that she complains.
(In these dark days, she more than proves her mettle.)
But it's a role (Russ knows) she was never meant for.
Weeks pass, sunk in his Morris chair most of the day,
Reading, writing, drinking cup after cup
Of tea. But Pauline—what does she do? Oh, she remains
Cheerful—when she appears. But more and more
She holes up in her room. More and more, she drifts away.

Weeks pass, up on crutches, step by step,
Inching toward a release from his suffering . . .
But more weeks pass, and anyone with a clear
Mathematical bent could plot the shape
Of the curve, could plot his progress and extrapolate:
Why, he'll be himself again in fifty years . . .
No, it's hopeless, the curse will never stop,
Any more than this air of gloom will lift, the pain abate.
—And no relief, no refuge but in scholarship:
Old dust of the lamp, live dust of a butterfly's wing.

Months pass, and like some new old man he's up on a cane,
But no end really to the sense of weight
On his hipbones, and no end, ever, to the pain . . .
Seasons drift by, once more the trees are great
Fountains powered by sap, hurling up vast
Frothing crowns of leaves that catch the light
And come down. It's fall. It's winter. It's the night
Of a neighbor's Christmas party, 1913,
And something inside him snaps at last
When Pauline is asked to dance. Pauline?

She who always danced so beautifully
Has lately been refusing all such offers
In deference to her husband's disability—
But this time she can't refuse. This *beau* of hers
Is white-haired Captain Rolader, age eighty-plus,
Who fought so bravely (if on the other, southern side)
Fifty years ago. He bows; she takes her place
In his arms; the pair of them begin to spin;
And oh, it's heartwarming, to see the ancient Captain
Turning with such vigor, so much pride—

And yet to see the blood-flushed pink awakening
Of Pauline's face (the girl positively *glows*)
Is something else, and all at once Russel knows—
Knows he can't do this to her. It's one thing
To have destroyed, with a single misstep, his own life;
That's something he can live with, if he must.
But to feel that he has taken his wife
Down with him, that when he fell
He took her with him, dragged her down to Hell—
That's more than heartbreaking, it's unjust.

And when, weeks later, all the weeping's done,
When the two of them face each other, one empty dawn,
After a draining night of broken talk and shared
Handkerchiefs, Russ makes a speech to take pride in.
Hoarsely he tells her, "It's not your fault, Pauline,
It's mine. I'm the one who pushed you away.
If only we could go back—go back and begin
Again . . . But some things simply can't be repaired."
And adds the words she longs to hear him say:
"I'm the one who wants to be alone."

*

A family of two, just as it was before—
Although it is no longer man and wife
But father and son—and everything is how and where
It once was, save that Russ in many ways
Now seems the elder partner. Yet if he spends
Most of his time in his Morris chair,
Like some creaky old man, at least *he* stays
Occupied (plenty of work to do), which is more
Than could be said of John; for the first time in his life,
He rattles around the house, at loose ends.

Although never what you'd call a sociable man,
When he'd lived in Storey, as now grows clear,
John had held a place in the community,
Which—much as he loves Old U—he lacks here.
It's an odd sensation, when a man's home
Doesn't feel like *home*. The days yawn before him,
Long and lax, lacking shape or plan,
And for all his discontent, it's not easy to rouse
In the mornings, to drag himself out of the house—
Not easy to shake off so deep a lethargy.

John cannot say it, but it breaks his heart
To see what has befallen his son.
Not just the accident—though that's an affliction
Beyond measure—but the boy's whole life undone:
All touch of the feminine gone, Pauline sent away,
And no friend left but Schrock (who, crazy from the start,
Daily deepens a chronic alcohol addiction).
If only Russ had chosen to study horses, say,
Or dogs, or monkeys—but who can recognize
Any brother-warmth in an insect's partitioned eyes?

Russ's career as a field biologist is done,
Gone before it began. All those sun-touched things
That formerly served as a counterweight
To his books and papers (streams, mists, dragonfly wings,
A breeze in the crown of a birch) have faded. Gloom
Settles in. *Your life has gone out*—that's what
John longs to say; of course he bites his tongue instead.
You've shut yourself up inside a walled room.
What father wants to feel, about his son,
My boy will be all alone when I am dead . . . ?

John bites his tongue, one day discovering
(Or acknowledging: it's been there quite a while)
A bump, or lump, where he customarily lays
The stem of his pipe. It's some irritation, probably,
Which ought to clear up in a couple of days—
But doesn't. He waits a few more weeks.
   And the thing endures, small but stubborn. Eventually
He winds up in Dr. McCaughey's office, where he speaks
Timidly, since it's never been his style
To complain about trifles: "There's a little thing . . ."

The little thing opens awesome vistas, which in time
Lead to a small excision, and days of vast
Uncertainty.
           And when *cancer* is spoken at last
And John Darlington's stomach starts heaving,
His first clear thought is, *But what will happen to Russ?*
Dear Lord, he can't bear the notion of the boy's having
Nobody to look out for him—no father
Or mother, no wife, sister, brother:
A man alone in a wheelchair, in a big house
Gone dark and silent as the tomb.

It's determined that the operation must take place
In Chicago. Not a word to Russ until the very
Morning of departure—and then an offhand
And abridged account (no point in adding one jot
To the burdens the boy already must carry),
And a return home four days later, his face
Bloated and wan, like some root vegetable
Harvested too late, and the pain far more terrible
Than he'd foreseen. He's not himself, which is not
Surprising—having left part of his tongue behind.

Cured—except his tobacco pouch has been taken away,
An absence that follows him everywhere.
Cured—except he can scarcely tolerate
The sound of his own voice, lisped and slurred
Around the missing wedge of tongue.
Cured—except he finds it painful now to be among
Any but his closest friends, and even in *their*
Company finds he has less and less to say:
Sometimes an entire dinner with scarcely a word,
Nothing but the scrape of a knife against a plate.

We know what we know, we move with the heart's blood,
Which tells him now—logic be damned—
The cancer's a judgment on his own life.
Of this John feels so certain, he needn't ask what crime
He may have committed, exactly, that would,
By way of punishment or expiation, have dimmed
His life's chief pleasures, given him a matchless wife
Dead at twenty-five, and a stillborn son, and a son who
Has become a hunched semi-cripple, partial to
The dry, measured speech of a man old before his time . . .

(Yet however richly deserved their damnation,
Hell's inmates go on plotting their escapes—and so
It's with some relief he hears Dr. McCaughey say,
Six months after the first operation,
"We didn't get it all." Oh? It seems the doctors want
Another piece of his tongue.

                      And this time? John says *no*—
Utters his *no* with all the stalwartness
A lisping man can muster. He won't
Go down unable to mouth a *few* words, anyway.
Like *Fare-thee-well, my boy,* and *Be strong,* and *God bless.*)

A few words . . . He begins that very night,
With a careful setting-out of his rationale.
They sit at either end of the dining table.
And John feels proud of how he brings it off: this time he's
Resolute, reasoned, and, above all, clear-eyed.
(He recalls, wincing even yet, the Pfeiffer Hotel,
The disastrous pre-wedding dinner when he tried
To speak about a husband's responsibilities.)
No tears this time: "We'll help each other. I'll fight
This thing just as long as I am able."

*

In Xanadu did Kubla Khan
A stately pleasure dome decree—
Its blueprints drafted, actually,
In a farmhouse in Somersetshire, bred
In the mind of a poet whose milk of paradise
Was an opium cocktail—ingested (so he said)
To ease his dysentery. In any case, pain
Had a role in another "miracle of rare device,"
This one compounded in the mind of a man
Whose cancer of the tongue seemed to press upon his brain.

In Indiana did John Darlington
A stately treasure dome foresee . . .
In fact, the vision began to unfold
On a stalled train, outside Indianapolis,
One raw, dilapidated March afternoon
When, peering out over a stubbly cornfield
And worrying, as ever, about his crippled son,
Who just might find himself, and soon,
Alone in a vast house—it came to John suddenly
That the house would never be a real home to Russ.

Russ's true home would always be his laboratory . . .
And then the vision rose: a great, gleaming limestone
Edifice, domed and pillared, spired
And castellated, the finest such structure
In the state of Indiana—and the crowning glory
Of the Campus . . . Oh, it all came clear! What was required
Was capital well beyond even John's own
Considerable means; yes, if his pretty picture
Was to become a fact, allies must be enlisted—
Old obligations called in, arms twisted.

(But why hadn't he thought of this before—
When, if you stopped to think, it was so obvious?
What was the *matter* with him? What else could it be
But his age-old problem—selfishness—
A failure to consider what was best for Russ?
    And sitting on the train, puffing furiously
On his pipe—a solace granted him once more
Now he'd accepted his death sentence—
John squirms at the thought of his own iniquity
And yearns to make amends, hungers for repentance.)

And the John Darlington who sets off from home
The next morning in his black greatcoat,
Jaw scraped raw with the closeness of his shave,
Is much the man of old, secure in his power,
Resolute in his purpose . . . He's off to "strategize"
With Dean Buchman on how best to mobilize
The Board of Trustees, how to give a gentle shove
To the President.
              It's been a matter of pride for him,
While building what some have called a business empire,
To request no special favors, to pay each note

One hundred cents on the dollar, and yet
(If you care to think in such terms) there's quite a long line
Of men who might be said to be standing in his debt;
There are many little "chits" he might now call—
Favors legitimately owing.
And this is the time to call them in, all
The debts of a lifetime, for it keeps growing,
The vision in John's head: not only library
And laboratory, but museum too: a shrine
To the living wonders of God's glory.

Setting out from home that frosty March morning
In 1915, John saw, with crystalline lucency,
That his was a race against time—or a race
Of one sort of construction against another.
For even as the pride of the University
Rises, inside his head, another structure's forming,
Also in his head.
                    This one's dark. Pieced together
By Satan's smallest minions. Who, cell by cell, put in place
A microcastle. Complete with sunless keep.
From which there's no parole, no escape.

Yet the white palace beckons: what an undertaking!
(Bigger than anything he's attempted in the past . . .)
Years, it would be years before the excavation
Was under way—the Museum's groundbreaking—
And *then* a construction to oversee, brick by brick!
(In truth, the size of the job made him faintly sick,
But good heavens, man, your life's work is clear at last—
Now, *Do you or don't you have the guts to see it through?*
It seemed he just might—no, it seemed he had to.)
And John consented to a second operation.

An Encounter

(1922–1923)

Angling through the skylight, wan winter sun
Encounters summer sun, ablaze upon the wall,
A rendezvous encompassing
Two hundred million years—the distance run
Between the pallid glow filtering through
The skylight, one Tuesday in December, 1922,
And the high-blooded meridional
Heyday of a Mesozoic marsh, outsize and lush
In this the Great Age of Reptiles, slithering
Out from under an artist's paintbrush.

Their designated meeting point
Is a new museum's Grand Rotunda, where, although
Its doors have closed for the day, two figures remain:
High in his makeshift scaffolding, a tow-
Headed young artist, struggling to paint
A neocalamite—a prehistoric fern—
And, across the Rotunda, a seated man,
A scientist, once as dark as the other is fair
(Temples now threaded with gray), who, from his chair,
Scrutinizes the painter's every turn.

The site-in-progress is the John Darlington Hall
Of the Natural Sciences, final brainchild
Of the scientist's late father. Yes, John's vision, born
On a stalled train in a midwestern cornfield,
Has gone up: a combination library/
Gallery of laboratories/repository
For a quickly growing treasure trove: a tortoise shell,
A mammoth's skull, a cavernous amethyst, a Viking hull,
A totem pole, rare butterflies, a Saxon shield,
The world's largest rhinoceros horn . . .

Russel watches as the artist, Hjalmar Gustafsson
(Whom he thinks of fondly as the Kid, or the Swede),
Reconstitutes a Carboniferous fern known
Solely from a few fossils. Yet these fossils, as though
Sensible to the rooting and rending need
Of Life itself, ramify: Hjalmar gives Life to stone.
And Russel loves, in the late-afternoon sun
After closing, to watch the Kid reconstruct a day
As fresh as anything last week, though it passed away
Some two hundred million years ago.

It will crown the Museum: the "Progress of Life,"
A four-part mural-cum-cyclorama, unfurled
Under the dome of the Grand Rotunda, each
Quadrant twenty feet long by twelve high,
A thousand square feet of life in all. Mural One,
The "Conquest of Terra," begins on bare Devonian
Shores, plants without branches or seeds, awaiting the world-
Changing invention of a light transducer—the leaf—
Then vast, vascular trees, an endless food supply . . .
And the land rush is on, as lobe-fins hit the beach.

In Mural Two, nicknamed the "Explosion," squat
Labyrinthodonts, the first true four-legged animals,
Scuttle through swamp. Towering scale trees yawn
Over huge ferns. It's hot. The air soars
With giant insects, winging to the Permian era
Of conifers and comely pelycosaurs whose spines bear
Outspread fans like great ribbed sails—
Creatures one part dragon, one part yacht—
Navigating down the millennia into the dawn
Of the Triassic and the true dinosaurs.

Mural Three will evoke the full flowering
Of the "Age of Goliaths" (and the advent
Of those other flowers, the angiosperms, whose blooms
Burgeon and brighten, competing for pollinators,
While breezes go laden with ever-richer perfumes),
Lunking across the earth like armored gladiators,
Spiked and scuted, underlings to a king
Of beasts that is no lion but a colossus
Larger than scores of lions—when pterosaurs so monstrous
As to make sparrows of eagles crisscrossed the firmament.

Mural Four (extant only in sketchbooks) contemplates
A planet wiped clean by mysterious forces—
Another mass extinction. The earth's a bare
Valley, down into which come shying early primates,
Low and tense, like rats with sensitive hands, and a bizarre
Brood of what look like latter-day hybrids:
Equine dogs, or canine horses; antlered horses;
Elephants furred like musk ox; flashing saber-tooths;
Huge flightless birds, burly as stevedores; gorilla-sized sloths;
And the first (stooped, hairy, squalid) prehominids . . .

Hour by hour Russ has seen the mural form.
Of course the Museum is "his baby" (has been since
His father's passing, two years ago),
And he naturally keeps a close watch
On all developments. In addition, his pride's
At stake here, for only at his insistence
Was Hjalmar hired in the first place, a decision which
Had all the early earmarks of a fiasco:
Up pops this queer kid who looks fresh off the farm—
A hayseed Swede who needs a bath besides.

But Russ's interest runs deeper than interest: it's awe
He feels at this chance to behold a miracle,
A daily revelation that does not stale:
The intricate reclamation of a terrain—
Each leaf and rock, root and egg—no man ever saw.
The notion is *dizzying:* whole geologic ages
Restored, the stone sheets of earth's own
Autobiography lifted out and its pages
Pieced together, puzzled through in an artist's brain,
From which at last they spring, breathing and full-blown.

(Nothing on earth, surely there's nothing on earth
So hopeful, so suggestive of some gilt, goaled kindness
Or mercy at the heart of Nature than the notion
Of convergent evolution—
This thought that the ranged obstacles to any birth
Are immaterial and can be sidestepped . . .
The eye, for instance—look how Nature kept
Contriving it anew, freshly seeing its way
Out of the darkness—as if, at the end of the day,
The mind were *destined* to escape from blindness.)

How gifted an artist is the Swede?
That's a zone where Darlington, heretofore
Having given the fine arts nothing more
Than a passing glance, is reluctant to proceed.
But clearly the Kid's no Michelangelo:
Even Russ can detect, here and there, a slight gap
Or warp in the perspective; clouds at the wrong height;
Streams like panes of glass, which never could flow;
Leaves so leaden the branches would snap;
A lizard's haunch that doesn't sit right . . .

But finally it hardly matters if Hjalmar can
Render a flowing stream, a flowering tree—
Trifling shortcomings, in light of the embracing
Fervor he brings to his task: clearly he's in thrall
To higher visions, and works like a man
Possessed. Up on his scaffolding, day after day
Lost in his own Lost World, he's creating, effacing,
Creating afresh—and a hundred feet away,
Across the great reaches of the Grand Hall,
You can *feel* it, the potent purity

Of a godlike ambition, a soul tuned to inner
Dictates the rest of us are deaf to.
And the result is, it's an honor, an honor
And a privilege (no other words will do)
To watch the murals form. It's Life itself, no less,
Evolving month by month—from the first clambering up
Out of the mobbed, mud-bottomed Cambrian morass
(Fins finding footholds, gills blooming like flowers to cup
The burning air) to the buoyant gentility
Of a robin singing in a cherry tree.

But how does he know? is the question Russ
Keeps asking, with shy but gaping incredulity.
How does the man *know* how big this cloud ought to be,
Or that boulder, on an afternoon that went down blazing
Two hundred million years ago? How can he *tell*
On which rock a lizard ought to creep, or a fern rise,
Which direction to make the wind blow?
Given how many byways beckon, all the mazing
Itineraries of the purely accidental,
How does the artist choose—how does he know where to go?

Even as the Kid doubts, reworks, replaces,
Knocks his head in self-reproach, pouts, pulls his hair,
Gnaws the wood ends of his brushes, fiercely erases
An hour's labor in a couple of seconds—it seems
He can see, finally, how he wants things to go . . .
As if, in the domain of pure coincidence,
He arrives at some firm *Yes* or *No.* But where
Does it come from—that kind of confidence?
A gift from the Muses? Does it spring from dreams?
How does he know? is what Darlington wants to know.

It's just this second-hand assurance—belief
In the Artist's belief—that has inspired
Russ to play apologist. As costs have escalated
And the completion date drifted further away
(For a year beyond the time allotted,
The hopefully titled "Progress of Life"
Has clogged and sullied the Grand Entranceway),
Russ has made excuses. But is the Kid even aware
He would have been discharged long ago—fired—
Were it not for the quiet man in the chair?

Russ has been dazed, and just a little shaken,
To witness at first hand so driven a show
Of industry. Amazing: a kind of monkhood.
Frankly, Russ wouldn't have thought anyone *could*
Pile up longer hours than he himself does
(For he's the man who one year, two years ago,
Made it to the lab three hundred and sixty-three days,
And relished the joke of having taken
More vacation time than might first appear:
After all, 1920 was a leap year),

Yet found the Kid would arrive before him, and stay
On after him, and sometimes (so Russ tardily guessed)
Didn't bother to go home—working all night
In this black vault of petrified bones. It was quite
A picture: the boy at last calling it a day
As dawn broke through the dome; settling down in the nest
Of the scaffolding, in his clothes; taking his rest
Under the open jaws of Earth's largest carnivore.
(In effect, Hjalmar's home was the Grand Rotunda—one more
Anomaly the Trustees hadn't bargained for.)

But there was another reason to temporize,
Compromise, forgive the Kid anything,
Indulge him in everything: that harsh
Unshakable cough of his . . . What could it mean
Except consumption? Like many a condemned man,
Hjalmar has mounted a final scaffolding,
There to paint for his life—putting heart and soul
Into behemoths with brains the size
Of golf balls, the kings of a collapsing marsh
That, eons ago, turned into coal.

Let the Kid work, that's Russ's motto, and mission,
Who alone among the townsfolk has declined
To turn *Hjalmar* into *Elmer.*
                                    What've we got to lose
But a little time . . . It seemed no one else understood
That while he looked odd (and, frankly, didn't smell too good)
The Kid just might be the noblest of them all.
—But once you grasp that the skull immures the mind
In an all-but-escape-proof cell, how could you refuse
This young man who aspires to turn a blank wall
Into a glowing, open vision?

On this December day, having logged a good day's work,
Russ allows himself twenty minutes to track
The rebirth of an extinct fern. Just before six,
He wheels to the elevator at the end of the Hall
And rides down to the basement and out to the back
Entrance where the chauffeur, Achilles,
Is supposed to be waiting. Not a Greek but a Turk,
Ironically, though endowed with his namesake's
Strength of arm, which can be handy when, as happens all
Too often, Russ-and-chair run into difficulties.

But today there's no Achilles. Darlington shakes
His head in weary chagrin and decides
To go out and scout around. He gathers up his file
Of papers and his cane, negotiates the heavy door . . .
An icy wind whips at him, his bare
Neck recoils at its bite, and Russel takes
No more than half a dozen steps when his cane slides
On the ice, nearly capsizing him—another fall.
His file of papers hits the ground and explodes before
He can quite right himself; his work is everywhere

And it's running away from him . . . Oh dear,
Oh *damn,* where's Achilles? Darlington stoops,
Frantically tries to pull things together, but they're
Moving too fast for a man with a shattered back,
They're off and running,
                              when, just then, out of nowhere
Steps an elderly elfin woman, wrapped in black,
Who, quick as a bird, scurries over the snow and scoops
All of them up. *No need,* Russ cries, *no need*
(He feels ashamed), and also, *Thanks very much indeed,*
And also, *Someone was supposed to meet me here.*

But all his contradictory, grateful cries
Are lost on her—so he perceives the moment she
Hands over the papers. There's a blankness to her eyes . . .
Oh: no English. In her long black shawl
And her long black coat, she looks like a Russian peasant.
He dips into his pocket, finds there (hang it all,
Where in heaven's name is Achilles?) only a fiver,
Pauses—extends it. Her gray face puckers, yearningly.
But five dollars? No, she can't accept such a present
For doing a crippled man a simple favor.

Damn it all, where *is* Achilles?
Honestly, the man should have been let go long ago.
(That's a task Russ puts off day by day;
He can't seem to fire anyone.) In place of money,
He draws a business card from his wallet, says, "Please,
Contact me if I can be of help in any—"
Sees by the tremulous, shamed look on the woman's face
That all spoken words are hopeless in this case
And writes—prints—on the back of the card, "Let me know
If I can be of help to you in any way."

*

Hjalmar was hired in the spring of '20. His commission
Called for "four prehistoric murals, each
Twelve feet by twenty, the work reflecting a belief
In the unity of Art and scientific Truth"
(The phrasing Russel's own). The position
Was awarded to Hjalmar, notwithstanding his youth,
Based on his apprenticeship with Charles Knight,
The world's leading painter of prehistoric life
(As displayed in New York's AMNH)
And a stickler for getting the facts right.

Hjalmar began in June. The contract demanded
"All murals complete within two years of starting date."
Hah! It's start and stop. It's amend, upend. Rethink, re-sketch.
It's ask to have the walls re-sanded
And resurfaced, because you've come to doubt
The base of your paint. (And then conceal
Yourself in a cellar lab for days at a stretch,
Drawing lizards, to "get the living feel.")
It's recast, retouch, rethink what was rethought . . .
The "Progress of Life" fails to do just that.

Fourteen months along, not one mural done,
Russ is called in to confer with the Dean,
Old Dean Buchman, who adopts an increasingly
Paternal tone toward the son of his late friend.
"Look, Russ, I'll go so far with you but no farther.
Hjalmar's on the next train. Let's be frank, you're the one
Footing most of the bills for this. You've been
The soul of patience *and* generosity.
But it's a bottomless drain. I won't let you spend
Another dime. I owe it to your father . . ."

John Darlington: apparently, they both feel a debt
To that noblest of men—only, it appears
Their debts now tug them contrariwise . . .
Well, if Russ has had a single friend, over his years
At the U, whom he admires without reservation,
It's good-hearted Orlando Buchman; and yet,
Like his father, Russ enjoys facing the man down
When the cause is right. With a cripple's exultation
In his own quiet strength, Russel Darlington replies,
"But I don't see how you can stop me, Dean."

No, Gustafsson's vision must be left to coalesce.
What did it matter—a few more delays?
Or another five thousand dollars, more or less?
The Museum was meant to stand from one century
To the next; it was a question of long-term worth . . .
(And the truth was, nothing else these days
Moved Russel so deeply as the sight
Of gawky Gustafsson laboring to give birth
To his vanished world: artist and artwork equally
Alit in the sun slanting through the skylight.)

Somehow Hjalmar's example led Russ to take a chance
On an odd proposal from a former student,
Now a publisher in New York: would Russ care to try
To write a textbook, an "intro to biology"?
Well—there were *many* reasons to demur:
Russ was no generalist; textbooks came and went
Like mayflies; Schrock disapproved . . . What's more,
It would only delay what clearly ought to be
His lifework: a compendium on the Lepidoptera,
Similar in scope to William Morton Wheeler's *Ants*.

Yet, confident in two hard years he'd have it done;
That some broader self-schooling might be replenishing,
Preparing him well for his grander designs;
And, all the while, drawing strength from the Swede
In his artist's aerie (feeling a humming sympathy
With the Progress of Life and its simple, astonishing
Premise that if you left a few algal mats in the sun
For—let's say—a billion years, they might eventually
Rise, erect railroads, cultivate sparkling wines,
And compose serenades for strings), Russ had agreed.

Besides, he already knew how the book must start,
With a line that cut its subject like a knife.
Gallia est omnis divisa in partes tres . . . ?
That's quite good, but better yet was *All life
Divides into two kingdoms . . .* No, he would take heart
From the wan, woebegone boy who was trying,
Between the coughing bouts that drained his face,
To do right by the joys of an earth that had, indeed,
Betrayed him—take heart from one who, before dying,
Meant to bring a world back from the dead.

*

[And Russel's words drift down the decades . . .
It's 1993, the scene is a museum
Of natural history (though this one's set
In New England rather than Indiana), and I'm
Standing before an exhibit called The Community
Of Life, when I hear an inner voice declare,
All life divides into two kingdoms. And yet
When I strain to summon up its source, the voice fades.
Fades—then comes to me, and the words, with their
Inklings of pure futility, sadden me . . .

It's hardly as though I feel any deep affiliation
With *Life's Kingdoms* by Russel Darlington,
Never yet having penetrated beyond the fanfare
Of its initial categorical paragraph;
But I know enough of the man's story to share
Some trace of the pathos in that touchingly
Mislaid confidence of his. All life
Divides in two? You almost have to laugh . . .
Would it were so simple, an earth evolved from three
Billion years of dicey DNA replication.

In fact, it's the burden of this exhibition
To show that life can be allocated
Into *five* kingdoms: plants, animals,
Fungi, and two varieties of unicells
(Even while acknowledging that this division
May not do justice to various "anomalies,"
Like the bacteria that live at pH 1,
A medium as corrosive as concentrated
Sulfuric acid, or the thermophiles that freeze
At temperatures below a hundred fifty degrees),

And for just a moment the wall
Of dense information laid out before me
Blurs and drifts away on a tide
Of vertigo, as I catch a dim sense
Of all the species in effect born in the years since
Life's Kingdoms was written: all those unimaginable
Creatures, flourishing in uninhabitable
Niches—a wild, carnival menagerie—
And still, early in the twentieth century,
Waiting to be discovered, named, and codified.

So it seems no exaggeration to say
It was on a rain-pricked afternoon in 1993
In a New England natural history museum
My *Darlington's Fall* had its origin
In a touch of disequilibrium—
A moment of dizziness stirred by sympathy.
Back then I knew little more about the man Darlington
Than that he'd suffered, when young, a tragic accident,
And that, prone to missteps, in his book's first line he went
Boldly and spectacularly astray.

Life's Kingdoms first entered *my* life back
In '75, a gift from an aunt in Surrey who,
Seemingly intent on establishing herself
As the family's leading expat oddball,
Sent me, an English major, a biology
Handbook outdated by half a century
To mark my college graduation. Yet the book,
Against all odds, stayed with me, through all
My moves, and sometimes I'd lift it from the shelf,
Reread the first few lines: *All life divides into two . . .*

And now a tug, pulling me away, drawing me down . . .
Of course I had no idea of the immensity
Of the undertaking, no sense it would mean going
On a pilgrimage to Indiana,
To pace the streets of Russ's hometown;
And twice to Micronesia, where Darlington
Underwent his tragic fall; and would take me (knowing
Far too little—wishing I'd majored in biology)
To interview entomologists in Washington,
Cambridge, New Haven, Ann Arbor, Urbana.

But my tale begins with that paltry little *pull,*
Deep within, and, deeper still, a slight *give*
Of uninformed consent—for who could've guessed
My project would lead me not only to the Midwest
And across the Pacific to the immense
Jungle of a flyspeck island but, at the last,
To Surrey and my aunt? Even so, there was a sense,
From the very outset, of the appeal
Of open borders; I felt a tiny titillative
Shiver in my chest; yes, here was something vast . . .]

*

Just after the New Year, his near-fall
On the ice nearly forgotten, Russ was paid a call
By a much-wrapped bundle of a woman whose face—
Wrinkled, fretful, friendly—he couldn't quite place.
Then he remembered: oh yes. She bore a letter
In her purse. Composed in an English little better
Than her own. This introduce Rosa Szumski. From Cracow.
Come to this country ago six month now.
A honest and hard worker, always clean, in need
Of job, full or part time. Either one please.

                                                                Indeed—

Russ decided to take her on, five hours per week,
Saturdays—though knowing this would awake
The wrath of his housekeeper, Miss Kraus.
(Russ was like his father in this as well,
Most at home with a housekeeper who intimidated
Even the "master" of the house.)
Unable to make himself understood, quite,
He set forth his proposed terms in careful detail
At the bottom of her letter, smiled, gesticulated,
And guided her back to the door—all right?

Not quite.

      "You think I'm running a nursery for the town?"
"No indeed, Miss Kraus." "I don't know how much longer—"
"Just so." "She can't speak English!" "Well—no." "And even
Brings along a bawling brat!" "I do apologize . . ."
(Apparently, Miss Kraus's formidable frown
Had scared Mrs. Szumski's granddaughter, age eleven.
In truth, this *brat* has a sweet face—red hair, blue eyes—
Perched on a body skinny as a coat hanger.
Maybe she'd translate for Granny? *She* spoke English well,
It seemed, though the child was so shy, it was hard to tell.)

ROUTINES

(1924–1925)

The trick is to find a routine and stick to it, just
As if all the time in the world were yours.
Let's say you're an artist with a bum chest,
Up all night hacking, lungs a sack of open sores,
Still with the rising sun you rise and set
To work on a cycad's trunk, determined to get
Its scaly bark correct, even though, long ago, this
Specific family tree vanished into the coal-press
Of the dense, fiery Carboniferous.
You—soon to be extinct yourself—owe it nothing less.

Or say you're writing a college text, a summary
Of the whole grand paleo-pageant of life, again
The trick is to soldier on, page by page, footnote
By footnote, just as though yours were not
A hopeless task, at least in this century—
New data, new findings flooding in
Faster than anybody can assimilate,
Thereby guaranteeing that every day,
No matter how you sprint out of the gate,
The finish line drifts further away.

No matter. If the trick is to find a routine
And stick to it, who could be farther
Ahead of the game than Russ Darlington,
A man who tunes his life—so adroitly—to the clock?
To the lab by eight. Work. Lunch. Work. Stop just short
Of six. Down to the back entrance, to meet
The chauffeur. Home. A quick wash, a fresh shirt.
At seven the usual dinner guest, Professor Schrock,
Likewise punctual, who takes the seat
Once nightly occupied by Russel's father.

All life divides into two kingdoms—well and good,
But each of them empires unbounded,
Vaster than anything Caesar or Alexander
Ever dreamt of . . . What exploit displays more mastery
Than the marshaling of a field like heredity
Or cell structure into a single chapter? Books are small
And the world is big, and who grasps its grandeur
Better than the man who knows he could
Devote a volume to one moth species and still leave all
Of its essential mysteries unsounded?

Russ would despair—or would despair
Far more than he does—were he not so impressed
By the Swede on his scaffolding, day after day
Coalescing a world in motion: Life pooling
And spilling from niche to niche, progressing and falling,
Like a breaker over an outcrop—over the bare
Bones of Mother Earth herself. Elmer's is the remotest
Workplace on the planet (millions of years away),
With no companion but a seated man across the length
Of the Rotunda, who watches and draws strength.

If they're fellow seekers, each in his fashion intent
On tracking Life's Progress, they have surprisingly
Little to discuss, as becomes evident
The night Russel invites him to dinner. Hunching
Over his plate, not quite managing to close
His mouth when he chews, Gustafsson shows
A tic never seen at the Museum: a deep, plunging
Nod that makes him look dimwitted. *Ja, ja, ja,* he says,
Bobbing like a clockwork cuckoo. It would be
Hard to say what's worse, the quick nods or long silences.

And at one point Russ, desperate to steer
The conversation down a navigable stream,
Asks the Kid a question that comes out sounding
Pitifully naïve: "But how do you know
What you want to paint?" A long pause ensues.
It's an invitation to be condescending,
But—worse—Elmer plays it straight. "*Ja*—I see it," he says.
Nod, nod, nod. "*Ja*. First in my head." It would seem
He paints only what he sees, although
What he sees isn't always what is here.

But if they have little in common with each other,
The truth is the two of them are companion
Souls—researchers of a Progress whose richness is
Undercut by a cruelly low survival rate.
Russ piles up his pages, and Gustafsson his
Layers of paint, one vision succeeding another.
(No less than rock strata in a canyon,
Those paint-layers evoke an evolving past.)
But Russ is thrilled when the Kid proclaims, at last,
The Third Mural complete—some two years late.

*

The test of the best routine is whether it proves able
To adapt, when adaptation's called for—
As when Miss Kraus, the finest, fiercest housekeeper Russ
Had ever known, one day announced that she
Had met a man (A what? A man? You can't be serious . . .),
And was moving, in a week, to Constable.
Ohio. Oh. So Russ made Mrs. Szumski chief cook (whose fare
Schrock in fact preferred, though she was far
Fonder of cabbage than any non-insect ought to be).
Now fourteen, little Marja could serve at table.

The problem with a routine is its way
Of concealing, behind the veil of day-to-day
Continuity, some slow, horrid
Degeneration. Such precisely was the case
With Professor Schrock. It could no longer be denied
That his drinking (a bottle of wine a night,
Minus the splash that, with a cripple's zealous need
For motor control, Russ took purely to be polite
But mostly left untouched) was ruinous. His face
(No prize to start with) had grown puffy, veined, and florid.

Likewise Schrock served as a cautionary fable
About the perils of meat-eating (at least
The bloody mountains he took knife and fork to
Each night on sitting down to table—
Russel would never dream, of course,
Of imposing vegetarianism on his friend),
Whose moral seemed to be that the fellow who
Typically comes to dinner "ready to eat a horse"
Will himself transform into a beast
Of burden—lugging the load of his flesh—in the end.

And there was—unignorably—an undertow
Of cruelty in Schrock's banter: half-muttered slights,
Offhand dismissals, glances of proudly patient despair.
Russ's textbook irked him, of course—all the more so
As it grew plain how long the detour it called for.
He wanted Russ's work to follow where
His own was headed more and more:
The study of lepidopteran parasites.
(Or, strictly speaking, parasitoids, since in most
Cases in the insect world, guest kills host.)

He accused Russ of "schoolboy sentimentality."
Of being "soft on the pretty ones" while turning
A blind eye to those others, the dark raiders—
The ichneumon wasp, the flies—that hide their seed
Within a host's eggs. Sentimental? Maybe so,
But a better alternative, surely, than learning
To relish such infernal ingenuities—oh!
It seemed to *please* Schrock when one of those foul invaders
Broke from a butterfly's egg. (You need
A sort of courage, sometimes, to reject reality.)

Too long had Schrock steeped himself in everything
That darkened or poisoned the world—what else explained
The man's increasing urge to shock
His listeners? Out of his mouth, like wasp larvae burrowing
From a spider's belly, the ugly words would crawl:
Off-color jokes, gruesome tales, gibes at puritanical
America, whose people had banned the "fruit of the vine"
(Slurring his words, meanwhile, in an unplanned
Display of the dangers of "a little wine"),
And calling Marja (just fourteen!) "our pretty Polack."

And then the night Schrock lost his last compunction,
Cast off all decency . . . For years the two men
Had joked that caterpillars were nothing but
"Eating machines"—ever-ravenous dynamos-
Of-digestion whose sole earthly function
Was to fuel metamorphosis. "Now tell me: if those
Are eating machines, what about butterflies? Hmp? What
Kind of machines are they, Russ? See what I mean?
Aren't the wings just a show? A sign to potential mates?"
(The girl, Marja, was still in the room, clearing plates.)

But would Schrock stop there? He would not.
"What kind of machines? They're—" And if Russel knows
What's coming, still he can hardly believe it when
The Professor—his mischievous, misshapen face shines—
Utters a word that perhaps has never been
Spoken in this house before: "They're f—king machines.
Isn't that right?"
                    It's as if parasites had somehow got
Into Schrock's vital organs: worms in the brainpan,
Larvae writhing at his heart. What else could lead a man
Who had dedicated his entire life to those

Fairest of all creatures in God's creation
To sully them like this? Why mar and muddy everything?
Russ was sentimental? Perhaps, but wasn't it far worse
To go through life without some touchstone
Of the sacred—nothing to hold off the disintegration
Of everything that's decent? No, by every means
At his disposal Darlington intended to cling
To the quaint notion that our Universe
Admits a few objects without flaw or stain.
Butterflies, say. Or a sweet girl, barely in her teens.

*

The trouble with a routine is its tendency
To give way abruptly. Even the best of them run aground—
As when Elmer failed to show for nearly a week.
Fearful at heart, Russ finally decided to send
Ned Callow, his personal doctor and trusted friend,
To the boy's rooming house. The doctor's report was bleak:
"I'm afraid we're looking at tuberculosis,
Russ." "You're positive?" "How could I be
When he won't let me near him—practically closes
The door in my face?" "Lots of nasty 'flu around."

Ned: "I have my duties. The boy's in bad shape."
Russ: "But he's begun the last mural. He's almost through."
Ned: "Almost through? Yes, I'm afraid it may be true—"
And a sharp exchange of looks. The atmosphere softened,
Though, when Russ poured brandies and asked his friend
To describe Elmer's room. Ned's eyes widened: "Well!
I had only a glimpse but—Russ, the place is wild!
Stuffed animals everywhere, and animal skins, piled
One on the next, bear skins, lion skins, and a cape
Made of honest-to-God parrot feathers on the wall!

"Stuffed crocodiles, a wolf, a stuffed kangaroo.
Skulls of every size and shape, and bones everywhere,
Those he's been drawing and those that were
Nothing but last week's dinner, still on the plate.
I don't have to tell you that the smell's appalling . . .
And he's got drawings pinned to the walls, to the bookcase,
Even pinned to the ceiling, Russ—so the whole place
Sort of flutters. And twitches, because it's all crawling
With fleas, top to bottom. You can bet I couldn't wait
To beat a retreat. It's a hellhole." Yes. But perfect too.

It's pity more than prudence, in the end,
Leads Russ to agree poor Elmer must be sent
Away for a while. It's painful to see the boy looking so
Gaunt, so feverish-eyed. The Trustees quickly arrange
A severance sum (Russ adds a supplement),
Money enough to get the boy to New Mexico
Or Arizona, to some salubrious place where,
Under a cleaner sun, breathing dryer air,
He can recuperate. Who knows? Maybe a change
Of scenery, a chance to rest, he'll soon be on the mend . . .

Elmer—Hjalmar—accepts the news with head bent
Low in resignation—or perhaps a grief
Too deep for words; it's hard to say for sure.
When the word *cure* is mentioned, his eyes burn,
Again ambiguously. Does he resent
What he sees as a show of polite dishonesty,
Or is he warming to the promise of relief?
(What invalid's heart fails to throb at the sound of *cure*?
What dying man doesn't thrill to *recovery*?)
He asks a few more days, to prepare for his return.

Comes a day, then, after closing, alone,
Sitting at the far end of the Rotunda, late-
Afternoon sun angling through the skylight,
Russ ponders Life's Progress. At some point you have to ask,
Where are we headed? The last mural's months away
From completion; or Progress is over, you might say.
For surely the Kid—who worked down the final stretch
Like a demon—sleepless eyes ablaze—determined to sketch
His ultimate vision—The Mammals Come into Their Own—
Will never return to finish the task.

One day the artist in Russel's life disappears,
And the murals stand frozen, and it's amazing
How empty the Grand Rotunda feels. And how very
Sad it feels—sad somehow like the thought of those
Herds of prehistoric horses dwindling to a solitary
Genus—Equus—and all the others gone:
Stout hypohippus gone, who trotted on three toes,
And haplohippus, and the horned titanotheres,
Doomed perhaps by teeth fit for browsing, not grazing,
And eohippus, the lovely-named "horse of the dawn."

The goal of Life's Progress remains in doubt.
But Gustafsson's sketch provides sufficient detail
For Darlington to guess what the artist was hoping
To convey. A clearing. Three proto-humans. A male,
A female, a scrawny infant at the breast.
Nothing sentimental to their little grouping—
No, if anything an enhanced ugliness in
Their bulging browridges, dirty sallow skin,
Sullen gazes. And yet the three of them—without
Becoming a parody either—somehow suggest

The Holy Family. The female's angling head,
Tilted like a tulip's, hints at a painterly
Grace: Our Lady of the Apes. Life's progress?
Where are we going?
                        Call it a warm-blooded mission,
A cupped tenderness, the flow of milk in the grass—
And a matching thirst for mildness, mercy, clemency.
The Swede's half-brute madonna was to be wed
To Giotto and Bellini and Raphael,
To the halo of something holy—glimpsed in a vision
Fledged, like those of many a saint, in a flea-ridden cell.

(Hjalmar's belongings? His stuffed crocodiles?
His kangaroo? His feather cape? His giant tortoise shell?
The wolf? The wolverine? And the immense, ragged piles
Of plans and sketchbooks? At Darlington's insistence,
All were crated up and stored in a cellar in the Hall—
A room concentrating a powerful smell—
Awaiting the day of the artist's return.

  Or awaiting the day when the whole
Mangy collection would be hauled some distance
Out of town and everything burn.)

A Better Mona Lisa

(1929)

Birds do it . . . bees do it . . . Call it the opening
Lines of a natural history treatise devised
By that other Indiana boy: Cole Porter.
Newspapers, magazines, Russ keeps himself apprised
Of the other's classy shenanigans. Cole coasting
The Adriatic in a yacht. Cole on Broadway. Cole
And Linda, his beautiful socialite wife, hosting
Royalty in London. Puckish Cole and a whole
Gaggle of giggly chorines rummaging
For lowlife in the Latin Quarter.

Lithuanians and Letts do it . . . Let's do it, let's
Fall in love . . . Another secret—one which none
Of Russ's colleagues would ever guess—that when at last
His workday's over, shoes off and necktie undone,
He's keen to tune in to the fascinatin'
Rumpus of Tin Pan Alley, conveyed across a vast,
Restless, jitterbugging nation,
Where it finds him deep in his "den," the lights
Low, sitting in the dark and swaying to Gershwin,
Kern, Youmans, Rodgers, and Berlin.

Sidestepping the chatter and slogans and announcements,
Songs spin and whirl. Their immediate source is some
Huge radio tower lording it over the prairie—
Dim red lights winking with imperial aplomb—
But their real source is New York, America's airy
Hotbed of ballrooms and showrooms, where skyscrapers race
To the heavens and the world's most stylish women dance
With the world's richest men. Everyone's getting rich, and Russ
Is glad about that; he longs to feel less gluttonous
About living alone in this monster of a manse.

It seems America's finding a new
Voice for herself—racy and catchy and clever,
Saucy and sweet—and oh, how Miss Pauline Beaudette
Would have adored the new tunes, and those ballrooms too,
Who dreamed always of a brighter *fête,*
Drawn to it with the advancing furry mania
Of a moth homing on a kerosene lamp . . . Russ's own fate
Was determined by a moth, *Urania*
Marina, bagged on a summer day in 1898,
And a thing of beauty is a joy forever—

Or would be if the world would just let beauty be.
But no joy in thoughts of fair Pauline, wings singed,
Bumbling into the woods on an ever-darker flight,
Stars blotted out and no moon in sight;
Merely to think of her makes him feel so sad . . .
Since she went away he's heard
Little news of her, but most of it bad:
A second husband in Pittsburgh, a third
In Detroit, and some sort of breakdown, finally;
It seems she came completely unhinged.

God rest his soul, old John Darlington
Saw how the land lay back in 1910,
Off to St. Louis to meet the Beaudette clan
And right away suspecting something out of true
With Pauline's mother. Liquor was what he guessed,
Which wasn't the case, but he'd got the gist:
A screw loose—a defect that evidently ran
Through the Beaudette line, including poor Pauline, who
Must have feared it all along, in that sudden
Despond she was prone to: the threat of coming undone.

When he can bear to think of her at all, he'd rather
Think of what he likes to think of
As the last time the two of them made love:
A pair of kids, nothing more, just a you and a me
(As the song would have it), a he and a she,
Rolling at night in a private sleeper car,
Bound for that ocean licking at the far
End of the continent (through woods where Kodiak bears
Waken to train whistles in their hillside lairs),
Two homesteaders in the land of each other.

. . . Of course life is no song lyric. And there were
Other occasions, after his return, after his fall,
Some of them failures but some successful—
He's a man still—but he won't dwell on those. He'd prefer
To think the last time he and Pauline came together
Was in a Pullman car—which is to say, the last
Time he made love to anyone was on the other
Side of the Rockies. (Just a young man, set to begin
His life's great adventure—but then his future got lost
Inside a jungle, and never found its way out again.)

And it was fully half his life ago
The message came to him by relay
That Miss Beaudette might not refuse a request
For a dance. It sounded like a joke, a prank, a dare,
Yet he dared to believe, and so believed his way
Into her arms . . . Half their lives ago, and who'd have guessed
That the second half would be so
Tough for them both, Russ more and more in a chair,
Pauline perhaps in an asylum somewhere,
And between those two young dancers not a single heir?

Wherever she is, she's—hard to believe—forty now,
And hard to believe his own face sometimes. Sometimes
                                        he'll catch
Sight of himself in a makeshift mirror
(Some sheet of metal in the lab, say)
And recoil in an instinctive momentary horror:
Who is that man with hair more white than gray,
And a face so knotted at mouth and brow,
Like a fabric in which there's been a tear
And a pull—yanking his skin into a stretch
Of pain even greater than anything he's had to bear?

And another secret, one somehow blended
With the music brought in on the radio: it seems
More often than not, these days, when the day's ended,
The displaced pain in his legs—radiculopathy—
Drives him to a state where no pleasure's so
Delectable as the thought of being pain-free . . .
His drugs *call* him. They ask him to join a slow
Dance through a field of waking dreams,
Where his mother twirls to Tin Pan Alley melodies
(And winged insects rise through morphine's metamorphoses).

Dragonflies, in the reeds, do it . . . Sentimental centipedes
Do it—as the mischievous little song
Crawls into his head and won't come out again. All day long
Cole's bestiary keeps resurfacing: the lyrics hum
And buzz, squeal and twitter and click,
Bark and whistle and gibber until,
Distracted at every turn, Russ finally concedes
Defeat and places a 'phone call to Mattell
(Latest in a long series of drivers), asking him
To come not at six but at four o'clock.

They drive west out of town, purely by whim,
Darlington at each crossroads reaching a quick
Decision and Mattell as usual posing no questions—
One of the reasons Russ is fond of him.
Other drivers have gone in for philosophy,
Or sought out business suggestions
Or (still more absurd) romantic advice,
But it seems Mattell's concluded that the price
Of employment to a lunatic
Is a high tolerance for absurdity.

Lately, sometimes, Darlington would swear
Mattell's got it right—a lunatic is just
Precisely what he is. He meets the first test,
Anyway, having lost all control over his thinking . . .
It's cold, this raw March day, twenty degrees
In town, colder out here, will spring never come? And what
Is he looking for? Darlington doesn't know—but
When he sees it, he knows it. There. Right there.
A cornfield, complete with scarecrow. And the sun sinking
Behind a distant, denuded row of trees.

The sky's a pink that once made Pauline cry, "Oh,
I wish I had a scarf, a hat, a pair of shoes,
Anything that color!"—words whose sheer
Ardor for life made his own blood sing.
He says, "This is perfect. Stop." And Mattell nods as though
Nothing were more logical than stopping here
In a cornfield heaped with snow. "I'll need the chair."
Naturally. Where else would anyone choose
To sit for a spell? "And a blanket." Just the thing.
"And maybe you'd best wait in the car. Looks cold out there."

So Russ is humming Cole Porter while seated
In a cornfield, rather than a dance hall,
And the truth is it *is* the most logical
Thing in the world. The scenery is suited
To his mood: the brown vegetal
Rubble, the stubborn never-say-die snow,
A sun too weak to cast a shadow,
And, for entertainment, a black scarecrow
No one ever bothered to take down—
A figure one-half specter and one-half clown.

All perfect—though rather on the chill side. "*Mattell.*"
And the next request succeeds in getting a rise
From the man's stone features: "Mattell, it's a little cool
Out here, and I'm wondering whether I might ask
A small favor. I need some whiskey." "W-w-w-whiskey? But—
There's none out here." "Perhaps there's maybe a bit
Underneath the seat? In your pocket flask?"
And it cheers Russ to pull off this little surprise—
To show Mattell that while his boss may well
Be a lunatic, he's nobody's fool.

So Darlington sits, contemplating the flat
Indiana landscape, sipping bootleg from the flask,
Shivering in the pale pink graying dusk
While a ragbag scarecrow gaunt as a wraith
Looks on, looks down upon him. Mattell's crude brew
Burns like hellfire, but not unwelcome for all that—
For it seems that in this regard, too,
Russ is his father's son: in his respectful fear
Of alcohol linked to an instinctual faith
That sometimes fire must be fought with fire.

Birds do it . . . bees do it . . . and so do gimpy men:
Facts of life he can no longer ignore or contain,
Something he must confront before it pulls him apart:
For how can you deny that you, too, have fallen when
You're in love to the roots of your hobbled heart?
In love from the crown of your grizzled head
To your all-but-useless feet? In love from the twisted line
Of your mouth to the tangled, torn nerves of your spine?
In love, in love, head-over-heels in love with red-
Haired Marja Szumski, who is just eighteen?

And if Russel knows anything at all
About himself, he knows he must maintain
Some semblance of control over the routine
Of his days . . . He's in love with somebody
Destined to move on—to husband and family.
(Really, it's amazing Marja has stayed this long.)
She'll leave *anyway,* which is why he must be strong
And make her leave; having confessed—to himself—his love,
There's nothing to do now but make her leave.
. . . He can't be forever waiting for the ax to fall.

He's been here before, had to let a girl go once before,
Which is what he did: he bade Pauline goodbye.
(Then he went off alone, to live with the loss.)
It would hardly have been right—wouldn't have been fair—
To ask a girl born to be the glittering star
Of every party to shine over the narrow route
Of his crippled days: like forcing a firefly
To spend its entire life in a Mason jar.
How do you say to a girl like that, *Let's sit this one out,*
When in this case *this one* means your life, no less?

*

Life's most striking aspect is perhaps its way
Of almost working out. We come so close. Many of us,
We come so close. Spotting some swaybacked old dray-
Horse in a field, consider—as Russ will—eohippus,
The dozens of branching species on the family tree . . .
What happened to them all? Where, along life's path,
Was their misstep? Not quite the right hoof? A design flaw
In a molar? It seems there's but one penalty
For even the most minor infraction of the Law
Of Survival of the Fittest, and that is death.

(The dead are realer than the living, insofar
As they alone sound the remotest notes on the scale
Of the irretrievable. They have their own
Music. There's a timbre to the simoom whistling
Through the eye socket of an ankylosaurus skull
No living creature can match; a rustling
Nearly beyond hearing in the feathers-turned-to-stone
Of archaeopteryx; a dim booming hum, bizarre
And regal and queer-comical, to the mastodon
Hung in the warehouse of a glacier, upside down.)

Darwin—the "Devil's Chaplain"—first perceived
Just how minuscule is the gap
Between survival and termination. If
One millimeter's added to a bird's beak, or one
Firming drop of calcium to its shell, the chain
Of generations may go on flourishing for
Another fifty million years. But one drop more,
One further millimeter, and the shell's too stiff,
The beak unwieldy; then the chain will snap,
And drop, never to be retrieved.

In Russ's own life, his studies are so heartening—
The life-passages of a butterfly are
So purely beautiful—as to be compensation
Enough, almost, for the waking realization
That only in dreams will he walk without a cane.
    The wings, a fraction of a gram, are light as air;
As light as light itself, the scales of the wing;
Theirs is a devout, disembodied zone
Where it hardly matters that his own
Body's broken; hardly matters, twenty years of pain.

In effect a man declares at the end of a day,
I've received almost enough—thinking *almost* should be
Sufficient . . . Yet one day the same man wakes and says,
*I have nothing—there's nothing in the world for me
Unless I have the one I love.*
                     And love?
Nature's revenge on the living, surely, her way
Of forcing upon us some brute recognition of
Our own depletion, incompletion, malfunction . . .
Love is the force that sees
The *almost* for what it is: extinction.

*

In his own life, his research makes plain
What few people on the planet can begin to descry:
How simple—at the root of Life—it all must be.
No nuance there, no shady ambiguity
At the base of things, but a simple, flat,
Peremptory *Yes* or *No,* somewhere a button which
Orders the organism, *Shun this* or *Pursue that* . . .
Something as simple as the shunting of a train:
You must remember, as tons of hurtling steel go by,
What shifts it all from place to place is a simple switch.

Russel has never had the leisure
For that glittering pool—that shining backwater—
Which is Philosophy; but so far as he can see,
And silly as it sounds, the "felicific calculator"
Of Jeremy Bentham comes nearest the truth, although
In truth even Bentham's seemingly
Simplistic division into "pain" and "pleasure"
Is too complex; when you get to the rudiments,
Going tête-à-tête with wasps or bees or ants,
It need be no more intricate than *Yes* or *No,*

An all-but-inorganic, magnetic reflex.
And yet—yet with their simple switches,
Their *Yes* and *No,* they erect and keep in good repair
Factory, nursery, granary . . .
How many human operations are there
Run with the smoothness of the mallard flock's
Unerring quest to the fountainhead of spring?
When it comes to feeding and sheltering
Its every inhabitant, what human city matches
An apiary's efficiency?

The monarch butterfly, whose eyes can see
No farther than a few feet off, will again
This year sponsor a billion-member migration
Through a world cloudy as milkweed.
It's the blind leading the blind
On a far-fetched, transcontinental odyssey
And somehow managing to find
Their destination; it's a system of navigation
To beggar Lindbergh's, tucked into a brain
No bigger than a grain of mustard seed.

What is Nature's nature? He conceives it best
Who sees it as that force in the cosmic night
Which, supplied with nothing but two buckets of paint,
A bucket of black and a bucket of white,
And asked to produce the Mona Lisa, will . . .
Will produce the Mona Lisa. And if only he were able
Somehow, scientifically, to express *this* point,
Get the notion down in some form that didn't suggest
A madman's raving—he could dine at Heaven's high table
With Darwin, Buffon, Linnaeus, and Aristotle.

It's a thought too large, too odd to identify,
Teasingly shimmering in and out of view,
Like trying to crack a safe: spinning the tumblers,
Listening, waiting . . .
                              The answer may lie
In the dots and dashes of a firefly's signaling,
Or spots and flashes of a butterfly's wing—
For Nature's a book, set in the language of numbers,
And if you had the code, you could read its lessons through.
That's why you work 363 days per year.
Because the answer's there. Because it's almost here.

*

He managed to do it once: chose to go it alone.
He can do it again. And yet—yet he'd been so young
Back then, and so certain he'd met the worst, he couldn't see
Just how desolate and ashen the world might grow,
Didn't understand how a curtain of gray
Might drape everything in time. Nor had he known,
Back then, how truly ruthless life could be.
Even as you mind your own business, working at your desk,
It will break your ex-wife, carve up your father's tongue,
Metamorphose your mentor into a grotesque . . .

The whiskey burns his throat, as it should,
Unsettles his stomach a little, which is good:
As evening robs the sky of its red and rose and gold,
And the scarecrow settles in for another cold
Night without either shelter or company;
As frost locks up a landscape that doesn't appear
To have settled whether spring will arrive this year,
And Mattell as he waits in the car no doubt thinks
With relish of the tale he'll tell his friends, over drinks,
Of the bug-man's latest lunacy,

Russ hugs his blanket. Bound, once, for those Malay
Jungles of boyhood dreams, Darlington crossed a sea
Gold as a trumpet, but today he's a man who
Hunches beside a hand-me-down scarecrow,
Sipping a moonshine serum that has him confessing,
To himself at least, both the potency
Of his love and his helplessness before it . . . No,
This time he hasn't the strength to let the girl go. He can do
Only the next best thing: pledge to count each day,
Until the one when she drifts away, as a blessing.

A Musical Suspension

(1930–1931)

The wise man learns to be grateful for
Those days when nothing breaks. To slip into bed
Knowing that the ceiling still hangs overhead
And the floor is still on the floor
Can be a comfort bordering on luxury.
Russ had arrived at a routine
And it worked—which is to say,
He worked; it allowed him to maintain
Fixity of mind throughout his lonely scholar's day,
Knowing the night would bring him company.

Each day the books arrived, or call them bricks,
The building blocks of a sort of Babel tower:
All those "explanations" whose sheer
Profusion—books on top of books, tier upon tier—
Threatened to overshadow everything
They meant to explain. And it was his job to ensure
The tower did not grow too high; he must fix
The materials into orderly piles—i.e.,
Chapters of *Life's Kingdoms,* in whose pages he
Kept the tower of man's knowledge from teetering.

And then at six down the elevator
To find Mattell gazing out with a pleased, haughty stare
From the new blue Packard, and be driven
Home in proud silence to Marja and Mrs. Szumski, there
To change his shirt, socialize, sort the mail,
And prepare for Schrock's arrival, prompt at seven.
Marja and her grandmother would serve the meal
And be gone soon after eight, Schrock staying later,
Until nine or ten, warming the bottle of wine
Inside him with a big "spot" of brandy. Things were fine.

At times, in truth, Russ liked to spin
Sweet private fantasies in which he drew
The girl still deeper into his life. She would become
His research assistant—noting whatever he noted—
Or he'd bestow on girl and grandmother some
August new title like Household Managers
And ask the two of them, yes, to move in.
    But Russ knew better. Things *worked*. A few hours
Of Marja at day's end, something to look forward to
From the moment he woke—was all he needed.

(*You know you're a true entomologist*
If—if after some thirty, dirty years
Of digging into buggy lives, one day, rereading
Fabre, you come upon the phrase, "Still damp
With the humours of the hatching," and your every limb
Prickles anew, with longing, as when, when you were just
A little boy, you read, in *The Three Musketeers,*
"Milady let one of those looks fall upon him
Which make a slave of a king"—and yearned for the stamp
Of a glance so brutal, beautiful, overriding.)

He loved her voice, its every syllable
Blending the timid and the firmly decided,
And the pale clement blue of her eyes (the color
Of a sun-bleached sky) and the rich red braided bands
Of her hair. But he loved most of all her plump, white, long-
Fingered hands, strong yet delicately seeded
With gingery freckles—hands of a faith healer.
He had no doubt those hands
Could have healed him, if what was wrong
With him had only been healable.

To watch her peeling an apple—*that*
Was a pleasure to revel in
For hours afterwards, an image to carry off to bed
As a talisman against the night's perils.
It seemed itself a special fruit—the rare palm
Of her hand—white as the apple's inner flesh, whose red
Outer dress sprung loose in airy spirals,
The blade's edge again and again coming up flat
Against the cushion of her thumb,
And never puncturing the skin . . .

In the back parlor, where Darlington never goes,
Stands a piano, from which occasionally is heard
A conditional note, a notional chord—
Sounds so errant, they're never quite registered
(They might almost be the stray
Tinkling of a hand slipping upon the keyboard
During a light dusting), until the night
When it suddenly comes to him: *The girl wants to play!*
   And when they were next alone, he asked her outright,
"Are you fond of music, Marja?" Shyly: "I suppose."

"I think you sometimes play a little bit
On the piano." "Play? Oh no! I don't know how to play."
"Well, maybe you ought to—ought to study it.
I could arrange for lessons . . ." "Lessons?" the girl replied,
Showing—seemingly—more bemusement than delight.
Had he made it clear? "You wouldn't have to pay,"
He added softly. Marja's head dipped to one side
And what she said so touched, so charmed him, he replayed
Her words over and over that night,
Alone in bed. "Lessons? But I'm too old," she said.

Too old! He was in love with somebody who
Wasn't yet quite half his age (and wouldn't be—
He'd worked it out—till 1934,
When Marja would be twenty-three
And he forty-six). "Too old! But you're
So young!" (Born the year before his fall.) "For you
It's all just starting! You'd have lessons here. Practice here.
After work. Say eight to eight-thirty, every day?
How does that sound?" Doubt shaded the girl's face—or fear?
    "I'll see what Grandmother has to say."

If not *precisely* clear, the old woman got the gist
Of her feelings across when, at eight o'clock, just
At the start of the first lesson, she began
Clinking and clattering every pan
In the kitchen. In other words she,
Who'd refused five dollars on a day when she was broke
And hungry, stubbornly spurning all charity,
Wanted no part in cooking up fantasy-fare
For a working girl. (The old woman spoke
Quite fluently, actually, with her kitchenware.)

And yet, in time, Mrs. Szumski too
Seemed to succumb to the earnest exercises slipping
Out from behind the closed parlor door—
Sounds announcing that the working day was through,
And a new sort of industry had begun;
Sounds originating singly, like the dripping
Of a leaky tap, but gradually verging
On a spaced band of voices in unison;
Sounds that fell forward when they fell, like the surging
Sprawling of a wave upon the shore;

Sounds over time solidifying
Into coherent, cornered spaces almost like rooms:
Rooms of a rambling house that demanded,
As all houses will, regular tidying—
Which was Marja's to do, who alone understood
Where everything belonged. She straightened the clutter
In the house she built, mended
The curtains, dusted and buffed the heirlooms—
Restoring to the glass an open glitter,
And a deep reflective polish to the wood.

The sounds were lovely, anyway, in the den,
To which host and visitor would repair
After dinner, one sipping, the other pretending to sip
Some brandy. (When the Eighteenth Amendment passed,
Ten years ago, Russ, seeking to be a sociable
Host as well as a law-abiding citizen,
Set in a "lifetime supply"; it went fast.)
   To Schrock's delight, Russ was starting to assemble
His chapter on parasites (a field where
Schrock shone; he'd served a dual apprenticeship).

In recent years, with dependable industry,
Schrock had made himself the world's preeminent
Expert on lepidopteran parasites,
Especially the minute wasps that prey
On larvae. "Old friend," Schrock would say,
"Be a boy no more. You're too old for sentimental.
Come to my field." Yet such reproaches went
Down so much more easily against the girl's gentle
Constructions—those ideal chambers where the lights
Blazed off the silver cutlery.

Marja made mistakes, it was true, in fact
A fair number of mistakes, but even from a distant room
You sensed the patience, the cogency, the moral uplift
Of this musician who so scrupulously backtracked
To set things right, to make things bloom.
And as for blooming, Russ nurtured daydreams where she
Emerged as some late-flowering prodigy—
His gift to the world the revelation of *her* gift.
Afterwards, people would say: The first one
To recognize her talent was Russel Darlington.

Well, she was no genius—it turned out—but a good deal
Better than not bad. Marja was "making splendid
Progress, given her age" (again, her age!)
According to her teacher, a Miss Mina Dole.
Day by day, her fingers scaled new heights.
—Russel hardly needed to be
Standing in the back parlor in order to see
Those hands as they climbed, corrected, turned another page;
He looked to them for comfort, as he descended,
Day by day, deeper into the world of parasites.

. . . If your gut hosts a two-foot guinea worm,
You must wait for it to climb up to your skin
And discharge its hundreds of larvae within
A bleeding boil. This is the moment to be firm,
To seize the creature's head, to wrap it round a stick,
To give the stick a turn—but ever so slowly, lest
Its body snap, leaving its hind end stuck
To putrefy inside you. A turn or two a day—
No more. And count yourself lucky. There's often *no* way
For host to free himself from guest.

The quiescent hookworm larva, which seems to know
When a better home beckons, is activated
If a bare foot crumbles the feces it lodges in.
After penetrating your foot, it makes its way
Slowly up your leg and attaches a fang
To your lower bowel, feeding on the ulcerated
Lesion of its connection. There it will grow,
And mate, and release a brisk new gang
Of social drinkers, who in time will thin
Your blood to water as you pass pallidly away.

On the other hand, the nematode responsible
For river blindness, daily flushing a fresh supply
Of two thousand snakelike larvae into your blood, makes
A specialty of settling in the human eye;
Whereas the *Taenia* tapeworm takes
A journey from a pig's gut to the human brain, where,
Home at last, it brings on seizures and psychosis;
And the elephantiasis roundworm will repair
To a man's scrotum, which proves capacious
Once inflated to the size of a basketball.

If you find a watch, you can safely hypothesize
The existence of a watchmaker—so went
Bishop William Paley's famous argument-
By-design . . . but what sort of Maker would devise
A world of such *clever* ruthlessness? Russ was face-to-face
With an old nemesis: his failure to disentangle
Life from various inklings of evil—and the more life,
The greater the evil. Ironically, then, the place
On the planet where evil came fully into leaf
Was just the one that most drew him: tropical jungle.

Maybe even the worst was foreseeable (so he saw
Best, perhaps, when the pain was bad, in visions fueled
By morphine sulfate) . . . Maybe all the worms, wasps, borers-
From-within are mere corollary horrors,
And, wherever Natural Selection holds sway,
Any niche, however vicious or vile, must be filled.
Maybe this was nothing less than the Way
Of the Universe—the Universal Law—
And no better life is possible: in all the jeweled
Heavens, no world where such cruelties wouldn't unfold . . .

If so, the difficulty's to explain,
Not abstractly but in spare
Cold calculating terms, the source
Of that human penchant for uncovering
Notions of justice, for viewing life as unfair.
What competitive edge is granted us, what force
Acquired through this collective hallucination?
How is the gorgeous hoax of Right and Wrong
Ultimately a tool of adaptation?
How are ethics dissolved in the fluid of the brain?

And the difficulty with the other school of thought
(The one that says the world isn't morally
Neutral, no, there's something else at work, true
Evil's loose in the world) is to explain
Its source—scientifically. Did it pre-
Exist life itself, roiled in the methane
Clouds of the Precambrian? Was it brought
To a simmer in some sulfurous Ordovician stew?
And how did it spirit its way into the nest
Of the amnion and the mother's breast?

Seated in the den, attending with one ear
To Schrock as he holds forth on the topic of ticks or fleas
And pours more brandy into that visage which
A horseshoe printed once, indelibly, again
Darlington's struck by a sense of how knotty are
His old problems,
                lurking in the jungle much
As a looped python lurks, for the chance to squeeze
The last sigh from your lungs, though now and then
Across the impenetrable canopy is heard
The modest vauntings of a songbird.

His life is in her hands—under her hands,
Played upon by her hands . . . He carries her music-making
Off to his bed, hears the scales slip and slide
Like a little steamer, chartered for legendary lands,
Plunged in the push-and-pull of deep Pacific swells,
Or a butterfly hunter on a slick jungle hillside,
Droplets trickling down each leaf and stem: it seems
Nothing, not even a black stretch of oblivion, quells
The music's roll; it plays all night, through his dreams,
Since it's the first thing he hears on waking.

(Sometimes it seems he dreams—or senses—*sees*
Into another zone where her hands are playing
Not the vast saurian jaw of a piano's keys
But the bones of his own rib cage . . . *Dear Lord above,*
To speak of losing her is like saying,
I'll carry on without my lungs, or heart, or liver.
And in his cared-for, caressive, calibrated doze,
Russel Darlington to a scientific certainty knows
No man who ever walked the earth has ever
Fallen so deep in love as he's in love.)

He tells himself her music in his head
Is money in the bank—as if he carried
An account book in his brain, into which
Each day's notes are duly deposited.
He must save up all he can, become as rich
A man as he can be, against the day when she
Withdraws, threatening him with bankruptcy.
                                          For one day
She'll shuffle into his study and—abashedly
But unstoppably—Marja Szumski will say:
I'll be leaving soon, I am to be married.

(He often thinks—can't quite manage to refrain
From thinking—of all the coarse desire she must stir,
How raptly the males in town must lay eyes on her
During her daily rounds: buying a pork chop,
Or a few onions, or—indulging herself—a day-
Old cinnamon bun . . . It's the closest he comes to a real
Hatred of his fellowman,

                   pondering the way
She rouses in them the longings she makes *him* feel:
The urge to touch her neck, drop his face on her breast, drop
Her clothes to the floor, one by one till none remain.)

So maybe he's setting up a store
Of new songs that will prove a comfort to him
When he's on his own once more;
Maybe each note of hers will serve as a keepsake,
Mingling with the music of tuxedoed Cole
("After you, who?") Porter, and with the grim,
Lovely "sob-ballads" of Irving Berlin ("What'll I do . . .
When I . . . am won'dring who . . . is kissing you?"),
All those motley musics of heartbreak
That keep us whole.

Yet sometimes, faintly, verged on sleep,
He hears another sound, a voice of warning,
And this one says, Russ, you've only made things
Worse for yourself. It says, You let her *deep*
Into your head and heart, and when she goes,
My friend, you'll be—bereft.
It says, Alone? Just see what the morrow brings:
When she departs, there will be nothing left
But gray expanses of unbroken mourning.
That's the day your life comes to a close.

ALONE

(1931–1932)

Yet when there's dying to be done
Sometimes the doing falls upon some un-
expected party. At dinner one night,
Russ's guest at table, Ernst Schrock,
Rose to his feet with a look of blurred delight
After stabling two plates of short ribs, some rolls
And butter, buttered beets, fried green beans in white
Sauce, some cheddar, a bottle of Riesling, two bowls
Of apple brown Betty, and a small block
Of peanut fudge, and thereupon went down—

In the broad arc of his fall
Seizing the tablecloth and pitching
Floorwards an explosion of glass and crockery.
    Green-faced, vast, supine, the great man panted
In pursuit of his life, while somehow Russ, for all
His pounding horror, felt cool enough to recognize
How insectlike was Schrock in agony:
Beached on his back like a capsized beetle, eyes
Bugging out of his head, and a mantid
Hand curled at the breast, twitching, twitching.

Marja ran for Doc Callow, who came with due speed,
While Russ knelt by his sprawled friend (whose good eye soon
Closed up with a little popping sound—
Or so memory later would have it, having need
Of surreal effects, perhaps, in order
To grasp the unthinkable). Still alive—but losing ground
Steadily: in the two days left him, bound in a cocoon
Of sheets—like a pupa on the border
Of life's most mysterious metamorphosis—
Schrock never crossed back into consciousness.

And weeks went by. It seems the earth—great mother-clock—
Swung on its axis, turning a cold shoulder to the sun;
Days went dark. Given how the old man had declined
In recent years, Russ hadn't expected to feel
The loss so piercingly. He had grown resigned—
Or so he'd thought—having already bade a dutiful
Goodbye to the singular Professor Ernst Schrock,
Who once took under his wing an unformed young soul
And, in a show of intellectual
Parthenogenesis, hatched out a son.

It's clear now the Professor always drew
So close, loomed so large, as to be properly assessed
Only in death: a man whose face was unbroken once,
In a boyhood perfused with its own radiance
And magic . . . One day young Ernst, chasing a blue-and-red
Pair of wings across an alpine creek bed,
Leapt and landed in the flat American Midwest—
Transformed into an odd, queer-spoken professor who
Finally shook off or scared off everyone
Except a little boy named Russ Darlington.

And maybe Schrock's sleep, too, had been troubled
By thoughts of Marja; maybe his leering ribaldries
("Our pretty little Polack") were admissions of love . . .
In any case, Russel now felt prepared
To understand all, to forgive the man all,
Since in the end their lives were nearly identical:
A triangular existence whose vertices
Consisted of Lepidoptera, a red-haired
Polish girl, and a staunch alliance of
The disfigured and the disabled.

Once, on a now-vanished field, strategic battle lines
Were drawn by two mighty men. One was the kindest soul
Who ever lived, yet someone who wore the shame or blame
Of the very world upon his shoulders. (His whole
Life was an ongoing apology, and his daily prayer
Might well have been, Forgive me, Lord, for displacing
So large a portion of the planet's air.)
The other, with his dented face, was someone to claim
Every indulgence as his just desert—the best wines,
The thickest cream, the sausage so plump it splits its casing.

And the prize they waged war for? There's the irony.
Here sits the prize—lined and grizzled—suspiciously
Eyeing his dinner and feeling unable
To undertake the task of lifting knife and fork,
Despite being hungry to the bottom of his soul.
　　It seems Russel required, after a long day's work,
A few companionable hours. To sit in the dining room
By yourself, lord of an empty outstretched table—
Good Lord, it was like being in your tomb . . .
And evening fell like a shovelful of soil.

Worst of all was the dinner hour, nerves unsteady
And unstrung, the grandfather clock's boom-booming grown
So much louder than before . . . He'd been a fool,
It seems, to have prepared no life of his own,
On his own. He *dislikes* eating by himself. And yet
Those friends he has, at the lab or school,
Are men who are married or otherwise set
In their ways—perfectly willing to break bread with him
Occasionally, but none of them ready,
As Schrock had been, to eat him out of house and home.

He'd *liked* meat on the table (though he himself chose
To abstain), and *liked* Schrock's sense of—lack of—style:
The way, in a rapture too deep for words, he'd purred
Like a kitten, growled like a bear, while he
Subdued his food. And Russ recalls, lovingly, the night
He glimpsed the Professor in a pose
Perfect for some painter's Allegory of Gluttony:
Sampling one dish with his left hand while
Reaching for a second with his right,
Even as his good eye fixed upon a third.

A few times, absurdly, Russ attempts to dine
With Marja and her grandmother—who clearly feel
Ill at ease in their new roles. Long wordless minutes:
Clinked spoon addressing spoon. Her looks suggest
He's battling one of the old woman's heartfelt tenets:
The able-bodied must accept no charity.
She's here to *work*. Does he honestly
Suppose she'd be content to play the guest?
Will she let herself be paid for sitting down?
—And who in heaven's name is going to serve the meal?

For relief, as his entire schedule falls apart,
Molelike Russel burrows deeper into the clay
Of his work—ever farther into the dark dead
Of night . . . What's the point of an actual bed?
He's been a troubled sleeper at the best
Of times and, these days, prefers to doze
In snatches on the cot in his study, in his clothes,
Waking at dawn and, yes, it seems another workday
Has arrived, Russ, and since you're here anyway, and dressed,
You might as well make an early start . . .

He says to himself, Look, you couldn't possibly ask
For better work; your study is the stuff
Of life itself: bio-logy.
He tells himself, Russel, you're at liberty
To go where you will, take up whatever task
Best suits you.
               Yet there's little relief
After something inside has snapped or let go
And the crippled man's become a broken man; no,
It seems even life itself isn't enough—
Quite—on which to base a life.

Sometimes now he'll let three or four days go by
Without a soak in the tub, a change of shirt—
As though Schrock's to be resurrected in this, too,
In his implicit insistence that the true
Entomologist ought to carry the dirt
Of his calling on his sleeve. What do you think
You're doing, Russ? an inner voice demands. Bright boy,
Don't you realize you're beginning to *stink*?
He replies: It's none of your business. You go away.
(Though who the *you* and *your* refer to, he can't say.)

He reassembles the bare bones of the tale:
A mother dead in childbirth (leaving her firstborn, age four);
A father lost to cancer (having initially
Forfeited a portion of his tongue); a wife who,
After divorce, passed from husband to husband (until
Madness claimed her hand for good); a mentor on the floor
(Felled by a stroke). Leaving: one Russel Darlington,
Partly crippled, mostly friendless, age forty-three,
A man hopelessly in love with a girl nineteen.
When nothing's to be done, what is a man to do?

Is it all in his mind
Or has the pain in recent weeks increased,
Until he can hardly focus on anything
But the prospect of sinking into a warm bath
Of morphine sulfate? (. . . where the upright semi-sleeper
Enters a twilit forest, densely crisscrossed
By the flight-lines of luminous, shimmering,
Yet-unnamed insects. Down one narrowing path
After another he pursues them, deeper and deeper,
Until the wings darken and the woods go blind.)

Let's say . . . Let's say, one summer day
In 1898 in Storey, Indiana,
An errant moth, *Urania marina,*
Bound for a rendezvous with a ten-year-old boy, sights
A rosebush . . . So: just a moment's delay, but the chain
Is broken, their routes don't quite cross, the boy will not be
Launched down a path that will suddenly give way
High in a Micronesian jungle; a calamity
Is averted because a haphazard cell ignites
In the micromaze of a moth's brain.

*

[So Russel darkly foreshadows a notion
Set to flourish decades after his death:
The idea, dear to the chaos mathematician,
Of the "butterfly effect"—Edward Lorenz's vision
Of a world wherein momentous, unreckonable
Consequences spin off from the tiniest motion
And a flap of papery wings in the Andes may
Portend a howling, deadly aftermath,
Summoning an eventual coastal storm that will
Kill thousands, thousands of miles away.

It's life as orbit-loops of caroming contingencies,
Chance changes, concatenated strings of events
Spooled through mathematical tapestries
Unglimpsed—unsurmisable—in Russel's time.
He was doomed to failure; it's the sole conclusion
You can come to, when you ponder our age's immense
Miniaturizations, the shrinking revolution
Of the silicon chip, and the indefatigable team
Of programmers enlisted to recast
The problems he addressed—as doomed as some alchemist

Grinding a mortar in a low-beamed hutch
On the edge of a medieval alpine hamlet,
A rolling-eyed madman racing to invent the wheel
On which gold's spun from lead . . . Russ had visions
Of discovering "how the chrysalis knows so much
In its sleep," of being the one to formulate
"The Kepler's Laws of food chains," of finding the proof
"That shuts up Darwin's critics."

                      I discussed his ambitions
Once with a young Yale biology prof,
Who shook his bearded head and said, "Well,

He's a guy with a sword, going up against a tank."
And yet our lame swordsman soldiered on.
   It was March '32, still in the dark undertow
Of Schrock's sudden passing, when Darlington
Was visited by some cousins from Grand Blanc,
Michigan, including seven-year-old Anne Marie,
Who would forever treasure memories of this
Grim, gentle uncle of hers and the hands-on show
He gave her (gave her exclusively)
Of a butterfly's metamorphosis—

A transformation no less capacious
Than the one from a pigtailed child to the whiskery
Whiskey-sipping orange-haired "old broad" (her term)
I encountered when I tracked her down
In the spring of '96. She was seventy-one,
Palsied with Parkinson's, and thickly, clumsily
Made up; I'd caught her with her "face half done."
She could hardly pass the biscuit tin she offered me.
Yet in that muzzy head her memory proved firm,
And her passion for the past tenacious.

Until now, I'd not met anyone who actually
Had first-hand knowledge of Russ Darlington,
And Anne Marie with a vivid gift for detail
Evoked the house in Remington, the meals, the den,
Russ's clothes and radio . . . She had a story to tell,
And perhaps I flatter myself, but it seemed she
Had waited her whole life for my arrival here;
She scarcely blinked when I pulled out a pen
And started taking notes, thereby transforming her
From conversationalist to interviewee.

"Uncle Russel spent most of his time in a chair,
Of course, but I remember him up on his cane.
You could see just how hard that was, wearing a big smile
To hide a grimace; even a child could read the pain
On his face . . .
                          He was beautifully dressed. I suppose
He was a man of real style—but a quiet style.
Nothing like mine!" She laughed gaily, patted her orange hair.
"And such lovely hands! When he handed you
A beetle or a butterfly, you trusted in those
Hands of his. And even felt the beetle trusted too."

Our talk unfolded in the knickknack-packed flat
She'd held for forty years. She had her own tangled story
(Married to a Scot in the RAF, who left her for
A French dancer and was struck down by divine fire
On his second honeymoon, when his Peugeot missed
A turn and met an oncoming lorry),
Which boiled down to a long childless expat
Exile in Surrey where—so she proudly said—
"Even the village idiot thinks I'm soft in the head,"
And where she served as far-flung family annalist.

"Uncle Russ carried such sadness inside. His back
Was a never-ending source of pain. And yet
The man couldn't have been kinder. He gave me a book.
Girl of the Limberlost." "By?" "It'll come. I forget.
But set in Indiana. That I remember. It tells
The story of Elnora Comstock. Who lives by a great
Big swamp and hunts moths. Which she sells
To scientists. *To little carrot-haired Anne Marie—*
That's how he signed it—*May the moths of my home state
Please her as much as they have me.*"

"How nice." "He gave me a book. Just the way *I* did—
I gave *you* a book." I draw a blank,
For a moment. "You gave me—" "The year
You graduated, Brad. From Harvard. In—" " '75. "
"Yes, I gave you a book." "You did indeed!
Life's Kingdoms. By Russel Darlington. And maybe I've
Never quite explained that that's really why I'm here,
I mean I actually have *you* to thank,
Because that book's the very thing that launched me
On my—" My? "—project."

                 Well, *project*'s probably

As good a word as any for my cross-bred enterprise,
Whose roundabout design should be plain
To you at last. Is my tale's genesis, the rise
Of *Darlington's Fall,* finally clear?
Anne Marie was my mother's aunt. And Darlington?
Russel was my great-great-uncle. What you have here,
Reader, is a remote family history,
Homage to an ancestor I never met, yet one
Whose buried hurt (*even a child could read the pain . . .*)
In time made its own enduring claims on me.

—Though as for this *Fall* of mine, my hope
Is to raise in it another sort of brotherhood,
Richer than linkages of marriage or blood:
For each of my triad in his way (the lepidopterist
Tunneling ever deeper down a microscope,
The poet probing a stranger's psyche, the muralist
Rekindling pure daybreaks along prehistoric shores)
Pursues an abstruse problem. Each seeks to say,
To a world rushing all the other way,
Stop. Remark this. Here are life-forms distant from yours . . .]

*

Not even the marching of Marja's scales,
Surmounting thumb-stumbling obstacles,
Can lift him up, when he's down this low.
In the den where his father used to sit and smoke
(A powerful, wistful man who rarely spoke,
Even before they took away his tongue),
Russel sits in his own sort of cloud—sits among
Gatherings of ghosts. Not even Marja's scales,
Nor the scales outspread on a swallowtail's
Blazing wing, can lift him up when he's down this low.

The dark's come, a season's done, and Ernst Schrock is dead,
Who worked all day and dined here nightly.
That man's dead who called science, quite rightly,
The art of asking pursuable questions.
    You have to know which road will bring you back—
And which one's nothing but a cul-de-sac.
Doggedness pays off sometimes—sometimes persistence
Is merely another way of losing your head . . .
And Schrock? A font of valuable suggestions,
Including: *Never ask the point of your existence.*

DARLINGTON'S FALL

(1933)

The notion of reaching a point where things
Can get no worse proves hopelessly
Naïve in most cases. Down a step, another, the foot
Pawing blindly in search of braced underpinnings—
Some eventual leveling out . . . But fate
Isn't through with you, nor is your searching done,
So long as you can manage stairs;
So long as you can manage stairs, there are bound to be
False bottoms, additional drops; it seems there's
Forever a further nadir, deeper down.

Or perhaps the process isn't complete
Until you're warehoused like a tortoise in
A ship's black unbreathable hold, flat
On your back and nothing left to do
But ransack your mind—
                                    Or until you float
Like a trig little beetle in the elegant well
Of a pitcher plant, your several feet
Scrabbling at the air for traction, your shell
Upheld by a steadily solvent brew
Fixing you firm as any collector's pin—

Or lying on the eruptive, violent
Floor of a jungle whose hymning flies,
Too close to your ears, buzz with the news
That the job was done right this time, you'll never rise
Again.
      The full circuit has not been run
Until you reach that juncture where you lose
Your last hope and cry out in defeat, *I am done!*
Done with life—whereupon Life, notoriously silent,
At last makes reply: *But we are not done with you.*
So long as you can walk, the descent will continue.

So: comes a day like a lightning shaft
And the blow from which—in shock, in numb-lipped fear,
In a wheezing panic—the suspicion
Dawns that all escape's impossible. The route
Is wired and the rules are clear:
The laws of physics will be obeyed
And our running debt to gravity be repaid
At last; the overtaxed stalk has no option
But to bend, and the candle caught in the sudden draft
Can, for all its leaping, only gutter out.

On the seventh of May, 1933,
The old woman, Mrs. Szumski, arrives on her own
To prepare his dinner. *But why alone?*
Where's Marja?
           She throws off a queer look. Her head
Rotates a notch. She says, "She not feel well." *Home in bed?*
Well, we'll just have to get along without her tonight.
A disappointment—but *we'll muddle through.*
Then a quick afterthought: *Does she need to see*
A doctor? Another rotation—or turn of the screw.
"No. Soon. She is soon all right."

And the following day? Once again,
No Marja. *But is she feeling better?*
Glg. Nnnn. (Swallowed sounds.) "Nothing you worry at all."
But for heaven's sake—what is it is the matter?
And now a different look, thick with a conspiracy
He cannot in fact construe. She says: "No worry."
                  And when
The Professor once more proposes a call
To the doctor, she shrinks and demurs—adamantly.
(Something in her stubbornness doesn't sit quite right.
And Russel is hard put to sleep that night.)

And the following day, May 9, still no trace
Of Marja, and no doubt about it, it's worry
Eating at Mrs. Szumski. She's grown hoarse,
And her face is drawn—as if she herself were ill.
It seems something just may be
Terribly wrong—but why does she look so panicky
When he calls for a doctor? Is she afraid of the bill
(Which Russ would be willing to settle of course)?
What is he to make of that wary
But beseeching look on the old woman's face?

What's the message in her quick, wrinkled eyes?
May 11, two in the morning, Russel wakes
In the dark and—like a switch turned on—sees the light:
That haunted expression?
                              This is *fear,* pure
And simple. Her look concedes what her speech denies:
The girl is gravely ill . . . All of this makes
Sense at two in the morning and he can foresee
No denouement but one: oh, Russ is sure
Where this must end: knows, now, that until tonight
He never faced the very worst thing that can be.

I must see her. It will not wait another day.
I will go to her in the morning, Russel swears.
And lies there helpless in the black
Hours before dawn, as he once lay
Helpless on a steamship inching back
Over the Pacific, a young man with a broken back,
Berthed underneath a low, sickly, green-gray
Ceiling whose paint kept breaking
Out in fever blisters—raw infectious sores
Whose edges were forever curling up and flaking.

Lay once as he lies now, in a sticky sweat,
Waiting for the dawn to break—
This fever to break—and feeling, in the maelstrom
Of his mind's making (a state like dreaming, while awake),
Dark anxiousness yielding to a bright delirium,
A knotted string of horrors: a coughed-up blood-plug
Flat on the mirror of the medicine cabinet;
A lice-faced doe in the ravine; Fabre's mole
Become a paste, which beetles carve up and lug
Home to a bountiful subsoil meal.

(Here's one more thing most people do not—will not—see:
When you die, the symbionts in your digestive tract
Do not die with you; no, that miniature road crew
Of stone-breakers, having broken down for you
A lifetime's meals, now prepares a farewell
Banquet, serving up the host they served so well
In life . . . Most of us shy from the fact
That even the most refined, silk-lined casket
Is, from their point of view, a bulging picnic basket—
Cannibalism claiming one and all, finally.)

One more in a run of sunless Indiana daybreaks,
Dim swamps of cloud, but Russ rises sharp at six
And, disdaining all hesitation, strips
And lowers his body into a cold bath. He dries
His limbs with a starchy, scratchy towel, ferociously strops
His razor, and shaves in swift strokes (then brusquely applies
A styptic pencil to a couple of razor nicks).
Puts on coat and tie, overcoat and hat, and takes
A fixed seat (while the mind races) in the den, until,
At the booming stroke of seven, he 'phones Mattell.

They drive a street they've driven many times before
Without ever slowing down. This time, when they reach
A certain rowhouse, Russ asks Mattell to stop.
He clambers out, says, "Drive to the corner and wait there,"
And alone, on his cane, makes his way to the door.
　　In the instant when his raised hand hangs in the air,
Becoming a fist, Russ feels he's about to breach
A secret, a deep decorum—or about to step
Into some Valley of Death. And then, heavy as doom,
He lets his fist fall: boom　　boom　　boom.

It's the old woman loosens the door a crack—
Pauses—then throws it open; and what is he to say?
Somehow, he hasn't thought things through
Even as far as this . . . She gapes at a—vision,
Visitor never gracing her door before today,
A man who looks this morning grim and blue-
Jawed as the undertakers he's descended from.
"I must see Marja." His voice, a low croak,
Unnerves them both. She eyes this apparition
On her doorstep, blinks, thinks, waits. "Yes, I've come

To see Marja," he declares, and with a flourishing thrust
Of his cane, he all but forces entry.
"You see—" Darlington says. "You see, I must."
He stands in a gray foyer, inhales a poor smell
Of cabbage and onions. To his right, a small
Parlor; ahead, a dark kitchen; and to his left,
A steep flight of stairs. He adds, "But where's
The girl, where's Marja?" and Mrs. Szumski's eyes lift
Upward, leftward—but how is he possibly
To manage such a flight of stairs?

How will he manage?
            This is how:
One step at a time, Russ, who grips the banister,
Plants his cane, and hauls his body up a stair, up a stair,
Even while the old woman is unraveling
Long bilingual protestations: a litany
In Polish, followed by pathetically simple pleas
In English: "No, sir; no, sir, no sir, please."
    But she—God bless her—is no longer someone he
Can afford to attend to, not with everything
At stake that's at stake here now.

A step at a time—one more—a steady climb . . .
He calls ahead of himself, "Marja, it's me, Darlington;
I'm coming up." And another, it's just a matter
Of proceeding one step at a time
Until—
        until his rubber-tipped cane loses its grip,
Slips on the wood, plunging him all but flat
On his face, as he hears the dropped cane clatter
Downstairs, *bump-bump*ing, and a note of anguish rip
From Mrs. Szumski: the cry of one
Who feels the earth tremble like thunder underfoot.

And now he's   on all fours   like some low
Animal, craned head yearningly staring
With a beast's dim yearning   up the bumpy slope, and now
Comes the moment to say, *I will not let them beat me, no,*
I won't be beaten. This is the moment to say:
You think I'm beaten, don't you? This is the time to say:
You think I'm beaten, don't you? This is the time to say:
You think I'm beaten, don't you? And the time for declaring
The unspeakable: *No, no, fuck you, no,*
Damn you, yes God *damn* you, I am not beaten, no.

Up, on hands and knees, no matter, up he goes
And whatever it is Mrs. Szumski's screeching
In Polish—protests or warnings—hardly concerns
This quadruped on the stairs, blood pounding its head,
Damming its ears; Russ keeps climbing. And upon reaching
The top step, struggles to his feet, finds himself before
A pair of doors and somehow knows it's *this* one, this door,
On the right, and *Marja,* he cries, *I'm coming in!*—turns
The knob and finds

             his darling:

                        sitting erect in bed,
Turns the knob and all in one instant knows

Everything's all wrong: he has misread the signs::
This is no dying girl.

                 "Marja," he whispers—prays—
But having completely missed his cue, bumbling onstage
Like some apprentice actor who stands under
The bright lights stammering, all his lines
Forgotten, mind a blank page—
Russ knows it's hopeless: no words could ever
Deliver him from this unlivable blunder;
No, he'll anguish over this one forever,
And *cringe* until the end of his days . . .

"Marja," Russel accuses, "you're not dying."
A pause. "I thought—" Her wide-eyed astonishment burns
His eyes; he looks away.
                              "Dying?" "I thought—well, you see
I somehow thought." There's a chair beside the bed.
Russ releases the knob and lunges into it. Sits. Turns.
And says, as composedly as he can, "What am I doing
Here this morning? One might well ask . . . It seemed to me
You must be very sick. I don't know why. I had—
Just a crazy notion got into my head.
This idea that: you must be dying."

And now a queer thing—indeed the queerest yet:
    Just the way a face in a mirror or a pond
Shatters at the touch of a rock, suddenly
Marja's face breaks   and the girl is crying
Fiercely, exploding tears. She manages to get
Only a few words out before new waves of misery
Undo her utterly: "Dying?" she wails, pained
To the point where she can only bark out a laugh
(A sound so despairing, it tears Russ's heart in half),
"I wish it—oh God, I wish I *were* dying . . ."

The girl buries   her face in her hands,
Her head in the pillow,   lost in her weeping,
While Russ, nodding like some bright-eyed dog whose master
Is reading to it from the morning newspaper,
Feels everything going over his head . . . He understands
Nothing, nothing as the sobs come ripping
Right up through the heart of her chest, faster
And faster until she can scarcely force a word out
And not even the most compassionate listener
Could understand what it's about.

(Yet he goes ahead and takes her hand in his,
As any gentleman naturally might
At such a time, sets it palm down upon
His palm-up left hand, while the fingertips of his right
Each seek out and settle on a knucklebone.
Is it the girl or himself he means to console?
He can't say, but he knows—as her body shudders with pain
And she calls down damnation on her very soul—
No hand was ever cherished as he cherishes
The freckled hand now laid upon his own.)

Bit by bit, in a ripped-up, sob-torn series
Of phrases, her story surfaces up from pain:
There was . . . she met . . . she met a boy (hers are sorrows
Shaking her limbs as if her bones would come apart;
Her breath scrapes—and her tear-tracked chin's like the heart
Of a broken-winged bird when you lift it, stunned,
From beneath the bright mock sky of your windowpane).
He works . . . Zahn's Mill . . . he made promises. He said—
Not that she blames anyone but herself, you understand,
But she . . . well, she . . . believed . . . and lost her head

Completely—she forgot the kind of girl she was.
(And Russ? Doing little better than she is—fighting tears,
While the hand she has given him is wrung
Like a rag.) Yes, there was a boy: and because—because
Marja *liked him so much,* she did what she knew
She shouldn't—and then trouble, yes her very worst fears
Confirmed, and when he went off, left her for good,
So ashamed, what could she do but find somebody who
Could fix things, so they said . . . But it all went wrong.
And the Lord punished her. As He should.

What could He do but punish her, who chose to send
Her baby away? And now it seemed—seems—there won't be
Another chance for her—for her ever to make good:
Because it went wrong. It went—and never—she
Will *never* have another, which was only right, only fair,
God's judgment on a girl who had sinned
As terribly as any girl could,
And if anyone thought she must be dying—why,
It was all she wanted, all she could ask for:
Yes: she wanted to die.

So hard to sort things out, given the racket in Russ's head . . .
One, the girl's been in love. Two, as atonement for her sins
She may wind up barren. Three, she feels there's a curse
On her young life—only twenty-one years old,
And all dreams of motherhood already dead.
Her mortal sin? Oh, he could laugh—
Since the best proof he has, in all the universe,
Of some sly, resolute Goodness at the root of life
Is the existence of Marja Szumski. Who lets him hold
Her hand in his. "Marja, you must listen," he begins

And pauses. "There is something I must say."
And Russel halts again. Fear's got him by the throat—
The choking suspicion that were he to stray
Even one further step, he just might lose
The little left him: some modicum
Of pride. What he now faces is the threat
Of a shame he could never shake off or excuse—
The worst: that of seeing yourself a fool
In your beloved's eyes. For he hasn't yet become
A buffoon for her, a figure of ridicule.

Not yet? "I've something to say . . ." Yes, it's all clear.
And simple. Just something a man knows, or feels,
When he stands at a cliff's edge and realizes
He can go either way: still time—he can turn away.
    Then Russ, trusting, as he must, to her face—
His fallen woman, awash in tears—releases
The root, the cane, the banister's brace,
Lets go of the last prop
                          and Darlington falls
Toward her, toward another teeming density: "My dear
Marja," he declares, "I love you more than words can say."

There . . . And his eyes fly to the window. *There:*
He got it out, and his voice, while thinning to a wire,
Didn't break. Russ floats, strangely bodiless,
Like a message in a bottle. He doesn't *dare*
Look at the girl, whose hand still lies
In his hands. Yet so long as he avoids her eyes,
He can give utterance not only to his love
But to his unspeakable desire.
But who could believe—who could believe
He would ever talk to her like this?

"I wake up in the morning and I think first of you.
All day long, in the lab, I see your eyes,
Your hands. I hear your voice. It's the oddest thing,
Marja: you've gotten into *everything* I do,
It's as if I'm looking at you even when I peer
Into a microscope at one of my butterflies.
And when the first bird calls at dawn, that's the sound
Of your voice calling—summoning me. Marja dear,
My entire *life* revolves around
Those hours when you come in the evening,

"And for hours after you've gone for the day,
I hear your piano-playing. Because the notes
Stay with me. Because everything you've said and done
Stays with me. You make a music as near
As my pulse beat, and the worst fear in my life, the one
That has kept me up more nights
Than I can possibly count, is the fear
That you'll decide it's time to go away
Forever, because—because although
I don't want to burden you, I don't honestly know

"How I'd continue if you left here,
How I'd live on with that sort of emptiness.
I don't mean to burden you—it isn't fair
For me to go on this way, oh, I *am* aware . . .
(And I'm sorrier than I can ever express
About all this. Will you feel any better if I say
I hate the way I am? Well, rest assured: I do.)
And I did fight this, really I did, Marja dear,
I'm so sorry, *I'm so sorry* to be saying this to you:
But I fell in love, I fell in love with you anyway.

". . . And truly the biggest regret of my life
Is having so little to offer you. Dear
Marja, if only you'd seen me way back when!
Or if I could start over—carefully. There was such
A *future* in my future. I would do great things,
Maybe, or anyhow make some life that would have been
Inviting to a girl like you, who deserves so much."
And now he must risk it: Darlington swings
His face around to meet her eyes, to dare his dare:
"Forgive me, forgive me, darling; I want you as my wife."

But no, no, no—not even yet is this sufficient: no,
He must spell out precisely the miserable
Conditions of the offer he'd bring her.
Make no mistake, there's nothing noble in it at all,
Nothing not finally traceable to his own
Needs and hungers . . . It's like climbing down and down
The rungs of a microscope, he needs her in every cell
Of his body, and—something most people don't know—
There are more cells in a man's little finger
Than people in the world. For life is as small

As that, and it is equally as vast as Love—
Vast as Love's kingdoms, which nobody yet,
Neither mathematician nor poet,
Has gotten the measure of.
Love's numbers are all but infinite
(Its chemical recipe begins with half a billion years
Of steeping in the swamp where life began),
And she must be shown his offer's not what it appears,
He must make plain there's nothing noble in it:
"Marja, dearest, I want to be your man."

*

Some twenty minutes after the room above
Grows curiously muted, the two voices dipping
To a murmurous impenetrable hum,
The old woman, tea tray in hand, goes slipping
Upstairs and, feeling like a visitor in her own home,
Raps lightly, then gives the door a gentle shove
With the edge of the tray. Of its own volition
The door swings broadly open and the scene presented
Is as improbable and enchanted
As any Old World fairy-tale vision:

Sitting up in bed is Marja, face aglow
But tears cascading from her eyes,
And sitting beside her, clutching her hand,
Is someone the old woman would scarcely recognize:
The Professor, his face, too, lit up behind
A waterfall of tears. Blindly, blissfully,
The pair of them sit gazing out at her
With glazed expressions, just as though
She were a stranger—as though *she*
Were the one transfigured here ...

The Professor scrambles to his feet.
"Mrs. Szumski, my news may surprise you."
He means to speak with dignity—but his knees are shaking.
"I have ... Marja has ... Of course, all such plans are pending
Your approval." The blush on the Professor's cheeks?
A schoolboy's blush. He says: "I've just asked Marja to—to
Marry me, and to my in—my un—my unending
Wonder and joy"
                    —wonder so potent he all but chokes
In its expression; his joy may be complete,
But his voice is breaking:

"She has accepted me. I—no, make that *we*—
We want, it's *we* are inviting you . . . My dear
Mrs. Szumski, you see it's our most fervent wish
That you would consent to join us. That we'd all be
Together. In *our* house. (I suppose I sound very foolish,
Or confused—I do know I'm not being very clear—)
But what I'm actually trying to say is . . .
Marja, darling, how do I say *home* in Polish?"
"*Dom.*" And now the Professor, recovering his
Composure, straightens his shoulders to declare:

"Mrs. Szumski, do say you'll agree to this
Sudden proposal of mine. Let's go *dawm.*" Oh, he's bent
The word out of shape—as Marja's grin makes clear to him;
Nonetheless, it's equally evident
He's saying precisely the right thing. *Dawm.*
A boldly gorgeous word, one without a home
In any language, yet the only sound fit to convey
His daring purpose, his dawning delirious bliss,
Precisely. "*Dawm.* Mrs. Szumski, it's time to come *dawm.*
With me and Marja. We'll all go *dawm.* To stay."

DARLINGTON'S DREAM

[Each year, we all excrete, I read somewhere,
Our weight in bacteria, although
Some of us do a little more than our share.
The march of events whose final goal
Was to steer me to a small hut in a vast
Jungle (a ring of pale dark faces—a kerosene glow—
The passing of a cup of stinging mud) was slow
And tortuous; but the path from there
To a rueful hunch over a seatless outhouse hole
Was sudden and direct as a pipe bomb's blast . . .

An offhand remark at breakfast to a waiter
At the hotel ("I hope maybe to explore
The Interior—of course I'd need
A guide") strikes a live response. Seems he
Has a cousin, up in the hills, knows every tree
And boulder on the island—nobody better—
In short, just the man I'm looking for.
Agreed? (In truth, I like the on-the-fly
Feel of the thing, the easy by-
passing of all tourist agencies . . .) Agreed.

Which is how I find myself fully made
Over—a one-man infantry brigade—
Marching behind Nat, a Napoleon-sized
General with ripped-raw insect bites and a striking
Gold front tooth. I'm wearing cap, glasses, polo
Shirt, seat-reinforced canvas shorts,
Wool socks with sweat-wicking Polypro
Liner (Eastern Mountain Sports),
Nippolo ("Hi-tech, hi-comfort"™) hiking
Boots, and a compartmentalized

Backpack outfitted with a first-aid kit,
A toiletries kit, three pints of water, four
Granola bars (Tropical Fruit), a Gore-
Tex® poncho, a Swiss Army knife, a banana,
Sandals, a change of socks, some Sun-ban, a
Compass, an inflatable mattress, a No-Kwit
Flashlight, matches, two spare Eveready
Batteries, a length of rope. He's wearing,
In brief, shorts. No shirt. Bare feet. And carrying
Nothing but rifle and machete.

It's easy going at the outset, a well-kept
And mostly level path, pretty much stumble-proof—
A good thing, since I'm all but swept
Off my feet at having come so far
To feel so thrillingly small, where fronds are
Bigger than I am, where the roof
Is cavernous and vaulted and many-tiered . . . Of course,
There's a war on, mate, as they used to say,
Yet it's the most inspiring show of force
Anyone ever put into play:

A land where, caught in a blaze
Of sunfire, churning ferns uncoil and fall
In colossal, chlorophyll-
Fueled detonations, where vines
Practice hand-to-hand ("twist and squeeze")
Combat, creepers parachute behind the lines
On search-and-destroy missions, and trees
Climb trees, burying each other in a never-
Settled battle for daylight that knows
No truce or cease-fire, ever.

I have an eye out for butterflies,
Naturally, those flower-powered ambassadors
Of a more pacific world than ours,
Never so much themselves as when they rise
Up brightly, just in time, from underneath
A bulldozer's crushing cylinder, or airily
Alight upon a steam shovel's teeth . . .
But I spot very few. And few
Birds, though Nat's rifle brings down two,
Little ones. He pockets them, literally.

The ground climbs. The temperature likewise,
With a whir in the air apparently one part
Insect, one part pure heat-hum.
The air, the light, the earth-smells rise
And fall and press a little closer and my pack
Hangs like a load of wet plaster on my back
And a small sweat stain over my heart
Slowly opens until it stretches from
Shoulder to belly—wet right through.
But we march on, who have a job to do.

Nat's English is roughly on a par
With my Ponapean, which ranges about as far
As the two-sided word of greeting
And farewell: *Kaselehlie*. But
Between the coming and going today I'll see,
He's promised me, "one cave" (he cups his hands),
"Six waterfall" (his fingers dance)—
No doubt completing
The circuit both hollowed out
And dripping sympathetically.

The path shifts, lifts, all but loses
Its way, pared to a low run
Of notched roots, worn stones, and now it's time
To take things in hand, half hike, half climb—
And suddenly hard to breathe, harder still
To see, glasses fogging over until, finally,
Going without them seems the best policy,
One which at least partly excuses
The couple of times I take a spill
(A scare, an ache, but no harm done).

The rain begins so
Abruptly, it's as if a gaping rip
Were torn across the sky. No cooling
First or exploratory rumbling,
No premonitory patter—just a free-
For-all free fall down across the tumbling
Firmament, and, at humble bottom, a pooling
Sense of persecution (as we slip
And slog) at having, everywhere we go,
A hose trained on us personally.

There's something just a touch lame,
It turns out, in standing before
A modest falls during a stupendous downpour—
Yet here we are. Nat wades into the pool
And I, my boots soaked through, do the same.
He steps forward eagerly, lets the thigh-
Wide column slap the crown of his head, and I
Do the same (a surprisingly cool
And urgent tattoo against the brain). So:
One fall down, five to go.

A site more splendid (nothing short of an ark,
Really, fishing us from the waters of the flood)
Comes when Nat, after another hour of mud
And rain, locates the island's—the earth's—lone
Refuge from the heavens' wrath: a dark
Snug cave tucked underneath an overgrown
Overhang. And now another of his tricks:
With startling speed, one, two, three, from the back
Of the cave he rounds up a pile of sticks,
From one pocket produces a plastic-wrapped pack

Of matches, from the other the birds, who,
Trimmed of feathers and heads, in just a few
Minutes yield up, with a rain-swallowed hiss,
Their two or three spare drops of fat.
Once blithe, now bite-sized, spirits . . . Nat
Seems amused by my pints of water. (I've been
Warned the rivers carry amebiasis.)
He finds his drinking fountain at the lip
Of the overhang, letting the deluge slip
Equally over eyes, mouth, chin.

I unbutton my shirt. Take it off. Wring
It out. Drag it back over sullen gooseflesh.
We sit in submarine reverie, listening
To the monotonous and ever-fresh
Music of falling rain. (The sound
Surrounds us, echoing off the walls.)
He asks, "Go more?" Well, what else is there to do?
   So it's out in the rain, up, down, an hour, two,
Another waterfall, and a couple more falls
Of my own on the rocky, muddy ground—

And another waterfall, this one a heavy-hitter,
Voluminous enough to roar
Even over the din of the downpour,
And finally a rest inside a leaky hut
(Abandoned), where I tape my blisters. He
Asks me, "Quit or go?" I'd prefer choice three,
Actually, a nutmeg-dusted cappuccino, but
In the end mine's the wan consolation left
To the recruit who will never be deft
Or strong: hey, I'm no quitter.

It's well past noon—a couple more
Poured-on pounded-on hours later—before
The rain breaks, and the heavy gray
Clouds, light as cobwebs, are swept away
Quickly—quickly by the sun's
Brisk gold broom—and all at once,
Between the leaves, something rare
(Rare and yet multiplying everywhere)
Flashes: can it be true? a blue sky?
    An unseen bird tenders a tentative cry

And the cry echoes, goes, grows . . . We enter
A sort of crowded clearing (plants dense
But low, no higher than our waists) and there
In the distance, wondrous and immense
Beyond all words: the Pacific. We must be two
Thousand feet up—open miles and miles of blue.
Nat's dark eyes and flashing gold grin declare,
Behold the planet's greatest ocean, and my
Island at its very hub—didn't I
Bring you to the earth's true center?

Night comes down sudden as a blow
Here at the equator, especially within
A jungle whose leaves ooze from their
Undersides squidlike jets
Of jet—but we beat it in,
Reaching a cluster of thatched huts
With some twenty minutes to spare,
Our arrival a matter of great moment to,
First, a ring of yapping dogs. I ask, "Who
Lives here?" Cousins, don't you know.

I'm led to a bench in what turns out to be
Both kitchen and dining room, on which I relax,
I.e., collapse, becoming a show of inert,
Comical fatigue—one that draws a big
And audibly appreciative audience
Of men, women, kids, cats, and one bumptious pig.
All quite comical—yet with a ghoulish ambience
By kerosene light (for there's no electricity
Here, which is the least of its lacks:
No walls, no floor; thatched roof, packed dirt).

But let the feast commence: Chicken in lard.
Eggs scrambled in lard. Spam (steak in a can)
In lard. Wedges of breadfruit oozing
Lard, bananas lightly lard-braised, and a snowy mound
Of rice. When in Rome . . . so I, like the others, discard
Directly onto the floor—onto the ground—
Whatever I can't or don't want to eat
(Chicken bones, a breadfruit husk), where the cruising
Vacuum cleaners of pig and cat and dog compete
To keep things spick-and-span.

I eat my fill, which leaves me more than full,
But Nat, despite his small size, once more
Outpaces me. I'm handed a can of Bud,
Another. Arrives now that gut-glutted sense
Of composure—one part stupor, one part radiance—
In which you feel right at home no matter how
Strange the setting; I'm at one with the mud
On my boots. A dog pants. Someone or
Something belches. Nat, taking a pull
On a can of beer, says, "Now try *sakau*?"

I've read of it, heard of it, you might say heard *it*—
Heard, throughout the island, the resounding
Beat of its preparation, the pounding
Of stone on stone. *Sakau:* a drug hazed in folklore,
Extracted from a native pepper shrub's root,
And the source, since time immemorial,
Of the island's most important ritual.
Amebiasis! cries a voice in my head,
But not the voice that currently has the floor.
That one replies "Why not?" instead.

I watch and yet don't care to watch too
Closely as one of Nat's cousins, whose English is good,
Reveals the process: the root's pounded on a vast
Ceremonial stone that has been elevated
On coconut husks to enhance its mighty ringing;
Then the pulp (its potency perhaps attenuated
By the dried grass, soil, and little shreds of wood
Crept into the mix and onto the menu)
Is cradled in the slimed stringing
Of a sieve of hibiscus bast,

To which a little water (cloudy gray)
Is added; finally the sieve's taken up
By strong (and in this case scab-encrusted) hands
And wrung until it trickles. Protocol demands
That in the business of the passing of the cup
Respect be paid to matters of rank and manhood:
The determination of who drinks when
Is crucial and complex. (My hope, needless to say,
Is that obliging, aging, formerly good
Midwestern boys aren't served till dawn, if then.)

Lofty, numinous, spirit-enhancing—
Just such as these is what the rite's meant to be,
Doubtless, but the best intentions somehow
Go awry and the whole thing hops the border
Into the outlands of cruel, Waughish comedy
When it turns out that drinkers One and Two,
The most venerable parties at tonight's do,
Can hardly hold the cup, for their hands' dancing:
Theirs the puppetlike tug-twitches of a (*sakau-*
Induced?) neurological disorder.

Stone pounds on stone—an ancient form
Of clockwork, bringing to a head
(*My* head) the moment when the cup tilts my way.
Slowly, shrinking, I close my eyes on a gray
Broth that resembles a generous scoop
Of swamp water, only thicker, and that feels,
Well, swampy on the tongue, and viscous, warm,
And *lively* . . . a bit like a soup
Lightly threaded with baby eels
Mistakenly presumed dead.

Cup follows cup. My lips go numb,
As expected, succumbing to the brew's
Anesthetizing pepper. I am struck dumb,
As expected, the drug working to uncouple
Brain and tongue. Another cup comes my way.
I bite my nonexistent lip. Another cup'll
Do me fine . . . No less than New York, say,
The jungle's a jungle, where you can lose
More than your way (for suddenly, in the green-black
Tunnel-ridden wall at my back,

I *hear* it: yes, the hunt's on, the fearful foray
In the dark, all the calculated, careful
Rounds of the preying and the prayerful),
And I need to pee. With a flashlight to serve
For both illumination and defense, I swerve
And stagger toward the outhouse,

                     and, looking up,
Find my gaze censoriously met
By a straight-faced moon, grim as a cop
Awarding you a ticket to your day
In court, grim-sober as a judge, and yet—

Yet a face, for all its severity,
That can't help giving the game away
Along the edges: silvery lines of quiet
Mirth on the leaf tips; laugh lines
Traced in the path's trampled mud; a comic turn
To the clinch of some pratfallen vines . . .
And when I catch him head on, lightly asway
In the middle of a puddle, his stern
Countenance collapses in a riot
Of uncontainable hilarity.

Then I—a weak-kneed boxer—return to the ring
Of drinkers, who are, apparently,
Fully prepared to go another dozen
Rounds. Me? On the ropes. Call it a TKO. "Bed?"
I say, and, miming, nestle my head
Deliciously on a pillow of air. A cousin
Of Nat's (or of mine, for we've become a rite-
Wrought fraternity) tenderly leads me,
Under Darlington's stars, to a hut's plywood floor. G'night,
I mumble, and extend my hand. Thanks for everything.

Inflate the mattress? Not enough air
In my lungs, in the night . . . I curl up in my bag—
And wake when someone drops both knees
In my gut. That's how it feels: a very tight squeeze,
Suddenly. I scrabble for the flashlight, drag
Myself up, stumble forth in my underwear,
Reach the outhouse just before a loud
Bomb goes off. I'm not feeling *well*.
Still drunk? Buzzed? What's the word—*sakau*'d?
Not sure. Hard to breathe in here. The stink. Oh hell.

And back to the bag. Back in—back
Out to the outhouse, and a sudden attack
Of the shakes (propped elbows lurching
On my knees, teeth a-rattling like dice in a cup),
Which pursue me back to the bag
(And a rush of sweat from every pore). Then up
Once more, zealously searching,
To my flashlight's lunatic zigzag,
Through an oversized vegetal maze whose goal
Is the frenzied fitting of hole over hole.

Then back—and back again—and a voice crowing,
This is no joke! This could be serious!
The Spanish have an expression, *To throw*
The house right out the window,
Perfect for an act of irretrievable
Extravagance. Well, here's a case of throwing
The body out the rectum—unbelievable,
Really, how many times I can give
My all, and still have some small all to give.
Then body-bagged once more, turning delirious . . .

Daybreak is misty, suitably so,
For I'm sailing the Febrile Zone, booked through
To Fata Morgana, where nothing's where
It's meant to be—the foggy here-and-there
Of a tropical fever which, two days from now,
A doctor in Kolonia will lay
To an allergic reaction to the *sakau*.
Or a bacterium. Or a virus. "You
Were sick—but now you're okay."
What else do you need to know?

(The twitching tubal writhe that keeps
Reconfiguring the sleeping bag is less
Like the deep imaginal flutter
Of the jeweled drop of jelly
Hidden in the husk of a chrysalis
Than like the rejective shudder
Of a tapeworm when a sheep's
Dismembered and its belly
Opened up: the blind dark-loving white
Worm curls, recoils in the light.)

Throughout the day I'm—bless her—tended to
By a big old woman in a vast
Red and yellow Mother Hubbard, who means
To revive me through trial and error. She fusses
Over a broad smorgasbord: cold baked beans,
Spam, potato sticks, breadfruit, some Hershey's Kisses,
A green orange, Doritos, a mysterious stew.
I eat a little rice, drink the last
Of my bottled water, settle back in
To my cocoon, drift in and out of my skin.

(And much as a mountaineer might exult
Over his altimeter (Twenty-one thousand feet!
Twenty-two . . .), I'm wishing I had the luxury
Of a thermometer to consult
(Have I broken a hundred and two yet?
And what of a hundred and three?
Where's the summit? And how will I get
Back down?).)
               In the clouds, I lack the lucidity
Necessary to the growth of irony,
So that, when it occurs to me

That I'm destined to die here, I have no notion
Of both how fitting and absurd's my fate
(Felled in the land of Darlington's fall).
It's just a fact. That's all—
As is the way I sleep across vast spaces
(Deep in the hold, bound across the ocean),
Beaching up, bone-weary, in the strangest places,
Deliriously begging a little water from
The locals, who turn out to be, each time, some
Mother Hubbard whose cupboard's on my plate . . .

And on the other side of the mind's mirror
(A misted wonderland of waking dreams),
I'm continually transported back
To a hot, hopeless hospital where,
Once, a shattered boy-man with a broken back
Kept waking to the same frozen nightmare.
(And in this gorgeous, godforsaken place,
In these my final hours, it seems
More than a comfort, truly a sign of grace
That he—Darlington—has never felt nearer.)]

*

Is he nervous? No. Pleased, rather. *Elated.*
And giddy-jittery as a boy
Before Christmas . . . Lucky, lucky beyond all
Other men, is the fellow who is "slated
To marry his true love on the morrow."
Father's words. And somehow the son's contrived to crawl
Up from despair and rage, fear, a crushing sorrow,
To reach this narrow ledge of dazzled joy.
So hard to believe . . . What does he feel?
Hard to believe his prospects are quite real.

Darlington lies in bed, under a moon
One day short of the full, mind in a riptide
Of frettings, fears. Will it all take place
As planned—truly? Dawn arrive, Marja at his side—
Tomorrow?
          Far out in outer space
The naked earth's spinning, quickly, the blue planet
(True blue), and he's on it—and she, the girl, is on it
Too, and yes the spinning dawn will come, will bring
A plump white finger slipping through a ring:
Marriage. Marja. On the morrow. Soon.

August fourteen, 1933.
Last night of sleeping forlorn as a ghost.
Maybe he ought to rise up, raise a toast
To that withdrawing soul, his Former Life . . .
Not a bad fellow, all said and done: true, he could be
Distant, dour, glum—but seldom one to fuss
Or grumble, and a good (if oblique) heart.
In any case, the fellow's scheduled to depart—
Simply no room left for him now that Russ
Darlington's about to take a wife.

Nervous? Not *really*. But now that he's down
On his back it grows so much clearer just
What all's to be done, how much he must
Still puzzle out before the dawn,
Mind   like the sea, propelled in robust swells
Home   toward shore, up from unsoundable
Deeps casting landward its imponderable
Emblems: labyrinthine shells,
Coins, bottled messages, a carcass or two.
So much to do, stretched flat: so much to do . . .

Nervous? *Yes.* Driven   with his head
Retreating down a sort of museum hall,
Legs chasing after and every footfall
Springing a *clang,* for now down what appears
To be a type of storm tunnel he's led
By the ringing of his running, *clang, clang,* and though
Sleep's impossible in all this uproar
Here & at last something lets him go,
Legs are his own, as they haven't been in years,
And he comes out upon a sort of shore . . .

Where a small child (a small child who can't be more
Than five or six) awaits him. Her skin is brown,
Like a Micronesian's, but in her hands and face
It's something other, perhaps a trace . . .
She extends, he takes, her tiny hand.
   All alters at a touch—and with the roll
Of footless ghosts, up and down,
Through junglish wonders, the two of them stroll,
He & his little cicerone, over the packed floor
Of a miracle-planted land:

Big bougainvilleas, erupting, and lemon orchards,
Grandly waiting, and mangoes gold in the sun;
Giant ferns, and clandestine fields of yams
On shaded slopes; a vast downed mahogany;
Towering top-heavy coconut palms
Aching to unlatch clutched caches of fruit;
Teak, ebony, and at the cataract's root
Angelhair mosses, fine as if spun
From the mists enfolding them perpetually;
Sweet stands of sandalwood, & orchids—

Orchids turned as on some master potter's wheel
To lapidary little teacups too fine even
For the most mandarin human lip—
Fit only for the replenishment of those
Who by the winged myriads come to sip,
To lap, to socialize and repose
(Who live on nothing less than ichor of orchids—
Thereby illustrating for us, in their odds-
Defying ethereality, the real
Mathematical likelihood of Heaven).

The path twists open, on another shore,
Though here the sea's a fresh-churned milky green,
And lime-white crustacea (miniature wriggling
Crab-creatures by the million) writhe and careen
In its seethe, knocking heads in the break and fling
And rake of a strengthening sea: a rising tide.
    His way is blocked: a cliff, like a locked door,
Stands at the end of the beach. Against its vastness, vast
Foamed breakers shatter, each bigger than the last,
And now—the one way forward—*he* must play guide;

So he hoists up the girl (the girl who has become
Scarcely larger than a parrot), and sets her firm
Upon his shoulder, and watches how the waves, caught
In a fury that never cools, assemble and explode,
Only to regather . . .
                        It's all in the timing. Just
As a wave's cresting, that's when you must
Scurry forward, advancing as the booming load
Comes tumbling, yes, Russ runs, he's in the clear,
The cliff rounded, another cove . . . He's brought
Her to safety, the bird-girl at his ear.

Now a narrower bank of shore.
Nothing but a frayed ribbon, really. A gray
Sand no-man's-land, between a swarming sea
And an impassable jungle. Yet the way
Is clear, his duty's before him, now there cannot be
Any turning back. And just as before, before
Him looms a surf-battered, boulder-
Broken cliff, but higher this time, and the waves grown . . .
Making certain the girl's still secure on his shoulder,
Again he watches, he waits, he makes his run—

To reach yet another cove. Another strip
Of sand. Ahead, another cliff, and one killing wave
Burying another. Truly, they never *end*—
His trials.
             Step by step Russ advances, assesses . . .
Then boldly springs, only this time the sea's
On to him, swirls round him, manages to trip
Him up, whirlpools round his knees, fights him—he fights—
Until he pushes through, safe, round the bend . . .
Only this time, it's not a cove but a cave.
    Up the round wet rocks he clambers. Light's

Odd here. Girl's flown. Catch your breath. Everything here
Skewed, somehow.
                    Still, shelter's shelter, you've won
Your way to safety (though you don't quite dare
Look round, not here, with everything just out of line),
Catch your breath, yes and maybe give a prayer
Of thanks, yes and attend to the sea as it rolls
Tamely through the rocks, the waters calm since you won
Your way to safety. Oh: ignore it: ignore the fear
Beginning to climb from the bare soles
Of your feet, down along your neck & spine . . .

But it's deep, deep from the back
Of the cave: where they come from. So: are you bold
Enough to risk it—lifting your eyes to the awl
Of an eye? (Tail's sinister slither? The quick
Light-licked snap of a tongue?) Behold them, then, behold
The dim cave-creatures out of their weighty sprawl
Summoned, by your arrival called from
                                        the black
Recesses, their big tumbling
                              torsos one by one
Unpacking themselves & spilling forward, quick, thick
As an ant colony boiling over in the sun—

And shooting low, some of them, humble niche
To niche, the little elvers too advancing:
Writhers & runners, all shapes & sizes . . .
 Ever so finely does Russ sense that the wall
At his back's independently acrawl,
The very rock he's perched on, *crawling* . . . Realizes
Ever so slowly this is that old domain in which
Nothing's not moving, and now at last he takes
The chance, and lifts his eyes (one glancing
Probe to the back of the cave), and of course he wakes.

[Once—I can honestly say—one time
I dreamed a dream in which somebody else not
Me descended into a dream, you may not
Believe this but I know what I'm
Talking about: one time you see I dreamed
Another man's dream—that is I seemed
To come as close as most of us ever are
Likely to get to getting out
Of my own head. I went far
Away, once. I know what I'm talking about—]

Or say he faced it down, and did not wake:
Screwed up his nerve and, for a lengthy spell,
Stared hard into the pit and did not break.
This is Darlington's dream—the dream as well
Of every naturalist since time began:
Of Aristotle's quest for the "coming-to-be,"
Of Pliny's "life as it is in reality,"
Of Darwin from his sickbed conspiring to seize
His so-called "mystery of Mysteries"—
The dream of mastering the master plan.

This is Darlington's dream, his widest hope:
No longer just the isolate detail,
The coaxed disclosures of the microscope
And scalpel, forever partial and piecemeal . . .
But now at last to sight the *res* in sum,
Fixing on Life Itself, on Life in Essence—
The quaint notion of the élan vital
Updated, squared with all the latest science:
To reach that more than metaphorical
Cave whence the whole animal kingdom's come

... And come in every guise: the deaf, and the bright
Ears of the aerobatic mastiff bat
That can, navigating thick woods at night,
Pick out the flight evasions of a gnat;
Blind, or accoutered like the dragonfly,
With twenty thousand facets to each eye;
Scent-deaf and -blind, or, like the peacock moth,
Able to track the dissipated path
Of the female's pheromone when thinned to one
Windblown molecule in a trillion ...

This is as close as he will ever come
To viewing whole the whole, to escaping place
And time—feeling the dark weight lifting from
The reconfigured bone mass of his face:
A painter's dream, this upsurge through a deep
Hunger that squeezes every nerve and pries
Open his jaws, as the air slaps his eyes
And the sun shatters and the lunging sweep
Of his head seizes on the fluttering
Prize of a pteranodon caught on the wing.

The artist in his soul, burning to make
A very world, no less, exults to know
No painter ever born, not Brueghel or Blake
Or Hiroshige, ever dreamed a tableau
To equal the fires of a Triassic dawn
Screened through the wizened gaze of a pterosaur
Nesting on a pitted limestone cliff-face—
A creature leathery and hunched and indrawn
As a baseball umpire until it uncase
Its thirty-foot wingspan, drop, start to soar . . .

And think of all the species hidden from sight
On this night when Russ Darlington lies dreaming—
Those whose reality will spring to light
In coming decades and will come forth streaming
Like the released-at-last cargo of the Ark:
Aeolian spiders (the sky's plankton), adrift
With the sere cirrus of the troposphere;
And tube worms fastened to the ocean floor,
Grinding out dayless lives beside the dark
Satanic mills of a tectonic rift;

Gold beetles in the jungle canopy,
Those glazed dynasties never touching ground;
And, based beneath a glacial mountain, gray
Inchlings spawned in an icebound rockbound pond;
Even a Malaysian lepidopteran
Outfitted with stylets for piercing skin.
(Russ might himself have been its author, had
Things broken differently—if only he'd
Not stumbled as he reached out for the prize.)
Ours is a world of vampire butterflies!

New species? New *orders,* new *classes*—new
Kingdoms! And word just in, even as I write
These lines, of could-be-organic residue
Pried from an ancient Martian meteorite.
Meanwhile, satellite photographs reveal
Ever more distant galaxies outspread
Like fields of sunflowers trained on that ideal
Sun which is nothing less than the mind of God . . .
And worlds within the whorls, birth without end.
"All life divides into two . . ." Oh, my poor friend—

Behold the helix, like a vine trained round
A spiral staircase long since dropped away,
A shoot flourishing free of wall and ground,
Itself its own nourishment and mainstay—
A kinked plait leading everywhere and nowhere,
For life goes everywhere (into the desert air,
The hot springs, ice caves, broken benthic slime,
The toxic sump, the steel-factory air vent)
And nowhere (ninety-nine point nine percent
Of species having gone extinct with time).

Contemplate the blind master architect,
With nothing more than trial and error—and all
The time in the world—contriving to erect
The ziggurat of a giant tortoise shell,
The leaning campanile of a giraffe,
The minute Great Wall of a coral reef,
A horse's back's suspension bridge, the domed
Mosque of the bull elephant, the unbound
Cathedral of a blue whale, the catacombed
Megalopolis of a termitary mound.

Never again will Darlington come so near
To seeing how it's all a sort of swap-shop,
An auction run without an auctioneer,
An open-air bazaar that goes nonstop:
The Great Emporium of Life-Forms, whose
Sole currency's a set of chits or scrips
So dense with figures as to be unreadable
Even to its barterers and bearers—strips
Of genetic information that compose
Both Inventory and Accounts Receivable . . .

Never again glimpse how it's all a vast
Casino with so many decks in play,
So many games, chips flying thick and fast,
Finally it's impossible to say
Who's in the red and who is in the black.
Another hand! they cry, *Another hand!*
The din's so great, it's all you can do just
To keep some hazy sense of where you stand.
(No one could be expected to keep track
Of all those who, without a word, went bust.)

This is his night for glimpsing how it's all
A bustling newsroom of an old-fashioned stripe,
With carbon copies, errand boys on call,
Scissors and glue pots, slugs and hand-set type—
A slapped-together cut-and-paste job raced
Into production, notwithstanding a slew
Of misprints, misidentifications, misplaced
Quotations, simple dumb mistakes . . . The text
Is corrupt but the presses roll; the next
Today's Edition's always overdue.

Each new day lands upon his doorstep like
A paper printed in some arcane tongue,
Bringing, it seems, war-zone dispatches (strike
And counterstrike, fierce skirmishes among
Redrawn neighbors), but who can say for sure
When even the paper's name remains obscure?
And yet it *could* be read . . .

                    Tonight's his chance
For glimpsing how Life's story might be put
In sentences, and every species but
A single word, with spelling variants.

(Though as for that, what gorgeous words they are:
Aurochs and oryx, gorilla and gazelle,
Ouzel and zebra, jaguar and jacamar,
Zebu and emu, lemur, philomel;
Saber-toothed tiger and scarlet tanager,
Golden tamarind, paradise flycatcher;
Langur and lamprey, quoll and quokka,
Thrips and thrush and foraminifera;
And the prodigal, sprung from winter's forge:
The yet-glowing ember of the *rouge-gorge*.)

(But as for that, what great plug-ugly words
They are: numbat, meerkat, muskrat, sprat;
Boobies and boobooks, warthogs and wattlebirds;
Milk snake, natterjack, muntjac, jackass; flat-
head catfish, wrasse, and trogon; grunion and pout,
Potoroo, rudistan, and red-necked grunt; black
Crappie, white grub, screwworm, screech owl; snout
Beetle, bettong, dugong, and stickleback;
Slug, quahog, dogfish, earwig, pug,
Pogy, pig-footed bandicoot, stinkbug.)

On all fours, if need be, a man will climb
A mountain—or a flight of stairs—to speak
His love; the broken body, too, in time
Must spill its passion or the heart break.
   But what of the soul—will it not insist
On its own declaration? His whole life through
He's longed to capture, capture and record,
Not merely the butterfly on his wrist
But the import in its coming—longed to construe
The text in which the creature's but a word.

In the beginning was the Word, and yet
Behind and underneath it always lay
A cryptic code, with its own alphabet
And lexicon, its distinctive way
Of joining and conforming thought to thought,
Its copulae and coinages—and all
These feverish intricacies figured in
A type font so elaborately small
Thousands, millions of letters could be set
Dancing on the head of a pin.

This is Darlington's dream: to grasp the deep
Grounds of the Garden, pattern of the Park
Where death lacks all purchase. In its full sweep
Not merely all the goods of Noah's Ark
(All creatures of the earth, the sea, the air),
But every one that ever was or might be—
The farthest offshoots of each family line—
Consort as siblings, each an equal heir
To the Domain of Workable Design,
The Garden of Pure Possibility . . .

To which, somehow, an interloper's gained
Admittance, one who can never feel at ease
Until the trees are trimmed, the fountains drained,
The paths revised—whose burning inborn need
To lay a shaping hand on all he sees
Is his peculiar genius. Or his curse.
The queerest tale in all the universe?
That of a brash actor who learned to read
The tongue his tale was written in and then,
Ignorant of the sequel, took up a pen.

It's there—*glory*—the unmistakable gleam—
Just within reach . . . But each time, his hands break
What thread or film it is that holds the dream
Aloft. It falls. Or flies off.
                                        He's awake—
Mostly—though his location is unknown.
He rolls over. He couldn't name the year.
Or say how long since he last slept alone.
(Sometimes he'd swear that she was always here.)
Still, the hand hungers, once more seeking out
The answer which—if fingers could not close
Upon a solid arm, or stroke the slight
Swell of a waist—he otherwise might doubt:
That he of all men is the man she chose
To lie beside her through the broken night.

Brad Leithauser was born in Detroit and graduated from Harvard College and Harvard Law School. He is the author of five previous novels—*Equal Distance, Hence, Seaward, The Friends of Freeland,* and *A Few Corrections*—four volumes of poetry, and a book of essays. He also edited *The Norton Book of Ghost Stories.* He is the recipient of many awards for his writing, including a Guggenheim Fellowship, an Ingram Merrill grant, and a MacArthur Fellowship. He recently served for a year as *Time* magazine's theater critic. An Emily Dickinson Lecturer in the Humanities at Mount Holyoke College, he lives with his wife and their two daughters, Emily and Hilary, in Amherst, Massachusetts.

A NOTE ON THE TYPE

The text of this book was set in Bembo, a facsimile of a typeface cut by Francesco Griffo for Aldus Manutius, the celebrated Venetian printer, in 1495. The face was named for Pietro Cardinal Bembo, the author of the small treatise entitled *De Aetna* in which it first appeared. Through the research of Stanley Morison, it is now generally acknowledged that all oldstyle type designs up to the time of William Caslon can be traced to the Bembo cut.

The present-day version of Bembo was introduced by the Monotype Corporation of London in 1929. Sturdy, well-balanced, and finely proportioned, Bembo is a face of rare beauty and great legibility in all of its sizes.

Composed by Creative Graphics
Allentown, Pennsylvania

Printed and bound by Fairfield Graphics, Quebecor World
Fairfield, Pennsylvania

Designed by Dorothy S. Baker